Write Dance

4–8 Years

Second Edition

Ragnhild A. Oussoren

A Lucky Duck Book

SAGE

Los Angeles | London | New Delhi
Singapore | Washington DC

This edition first published 2010
First edition published 2000, reprinted in 2005, 2006, 2007, 2008, 2009

First published 1994, The Netherlands

SAGE Publications
1 Oliver's Yard
55 City Road
London EC1Y 1SP

SAGE Publications Inc.
2455 Teller Road
Thousand Oaks, California 91320

SAGE Publications India Pvt Ltd
B 1/I 1 Mohan Cooperative Industrial Area
Mathura Road, Post Bag 7
New Delhi 110 044

SAGE Publications Asia-Pacific Pte Ltd
33 Pekin Street #02-01
Far East Square, Singapore 048763

Text and illustrations: Ragnhild A. Oussoren

CD
Music: Christan Grotenbreg
Recorded at: Lokaal 47 Musiekproducties, Rheden
Professional singer: Nicoline van Doorn
Young singers who volunteered: Adewura and Adeogo Adeiye, Samuel and Eleanor Bailey, Jenny and Rosie Sanders, Erde Weening

DVD
Produced by Ragnhild A. Oussoren
Camera and editing: Frits Boersma, Timeline Video, Groningen, The Netherlands

Library of Congress Control Number 2009941308

British Library Cataloguing in Publication data
A catalogue record for this book is available from the British Library

ISBN 978-1-84860-690-6
ISBN 978-1-84860-691-3 (pbk)

Typeset by Dorwyn, Wells, Somerset, UK
Printed on paper from sustainable resources
Printed in India by Replika Press Pvt Ltd

For my daughter Ariane,
we took the first Write Dance steps together.

Write Dance 2nd edition

Ragnhild A. Oussoren

Ragnhild A. Oussoren

Contents

Copy sheets can be printed from the SAGE website
www.uk.sagepub.com/writeDance2

After 15 years the book of **Write Dance** *was ready to be revised and updated.*

In the meantime two other books were added to the Write Dance Series: **Write Dance in the Early Years** *(first published as* **Write Dance in the Nursery***) and* **More Write Dance***. The second edition of* **Write Dance** *fits in between those two books. The three books, although they can be used separately, belong together and create a continuous line from scrimbling via write drawing to writing.*

For this new edition of **Write Dance** *the well-known music themes, from Volcano to Mandala, have been completely rewritten, and the music has been renewed. Nine variation themes, from Rocket to Rosette, have also been added.*

In the second edition of **Write Dance** *we still focus mainly on big movements with both hands, but we also progress towards the development of fine motor skills and working with the preferred hand.*

Each music theme presents a new experience with challenges to motor skills, expression and creativity, so that children will become familiar with the foundation movements that are so important for learning to write in a playful and natural way.

Ragnhild A. Oussoren

Fellow Write Dance practitioners and enthusiasts will be delighted with Ragnhild's revised edition of Write Dance. This edition provides us with an insight into the philosophy and the theory of graphology that underpins the Write Dance principles and the approach. The theoretical aspect has been written in an accessible style illustrating the impact that the social and emotional aspects of children's development can have on the progress that young people make when learning to write. Graphology is one way to interpret children's emotions and so-called 'personality traits'. Regardless of the readers' own views on whether this is a valid interpretation or not, what is clear is that the children are able to express themselves in a creative manner in response to the music, to the dance themes, and to the ideas for writing, drawing and mark-making. This emphasis on creativity, imagination, and playful fun is characteristic of Write Dance.

The references to graphology theory are not intended to replace the full teaching of the discipline; rather these explain the motivation and the thinking behind the Write Dance songs, music and movements.

The references are incorporated into the revised layout that now graphically illustrates the description of the movements and the teaching opportunities that are suggested by Ragnhild, which range from guided visualisation and story-telling to full-scale musical productions with costumes and props.

Most Write Dance practitioners will recognise many familiar aspects and themes; however they will also welcome this revised edition because the new material will enhance and extend current work and re-stimulate their enjoyment and enthusiasm. New converts to Write Dance will be delighted to see the illustrations and the descriptions that guide the teaching and inform the practice.

The Scandinavian influence is evident in Ragnhild's work; her imaginary 'Write Dance Land' is reminiscent of the writing and illustrations of Tove Jansson's children's stories, 'Finn Family Moomintroll'.

Ragnhild's humour and her vivid imagination stimulate this fantasy land. This in turn excites and motivates children to relax and enjoy the learning and the development required to master the physical skill of handwriting that frequently challenges young children.

I have no doubt that everyone who becomes involved with Write Dance will find this new edition a fantastic resource to pick up and use with confidence and enthusiasm.

Diana Strauss
Setting Improvement Partner, Early Years SENCO and Write Dance Trainer

One day on a long walk in the mountains I met a kind lady with a playful black and white flecked dog that placed a stick in front of my feet the moment it saw me. At first I thought that maybe the dog was lost, but fortunately I soon saw its mistress walking towards me. We briefly talked about the nature around us, the weather and her dog as we continued our walk together. Suddenly she began to tell me about little people that lived in a village deep, deep in the highest mountains, where hardly anybody had ever been. They call themselves Write Dance people.

The Write Dance people are naturally cheerful, musical and very creative. They walk very elegantly; it's as if they hardly touch the ground and are dancing all the time. They cover the walls of their houses with light terracotta coloured clay to seal holes and gaps, to keep warmth in and cold out, but also to be able to paint on them.

Around their village you will find long deep caves with white limestone. The Write Dance people stamp on the large chunks of limestone for such a long time that it becomes a very fine white powder. They mix this powdered chalk with dyes they have taken from various barks, plants, mosses and flowers and they turn it into a thick paste or a kind of paint. You need about eight large spoonfuls of powder to fill a small jar of paint, a little bit of water, sunflower oil and the yoke of one egg. All Write Dance houses appear to have a small cupboard with pots of paste paint in as many as thirty different colours.

Of course the Write Dance people have their own language but they don't know many letters. All their experiences are put into song and dance, and they are painted and drawn on the walls of the houses. These are usually pictures and representations of nature, or their surroundings, and of people and animals. When you enter a Write Dance house you only need to look around you and you know what is happening and what has previously happened in the house. They have even painted characters on the wooden doors and shutters, framed by wonderful movements of lines. Each family have their own flowery patterns and they are continually adding new ones.

How do you paint stories on the walls? Well, first draw some lines with a piece of charcoal, taken from a fire and then colour the figures by dipping a finger into one of the many pots of paint. Sometimes it may take you days. If you really want to let your fingers dance, then you ask if somebody would like to sing or wouldn't mind playing on a home-made musical instrument. Depending on the rhythm of the music you will make straight or round movements, which can be decorated with paints later. The Write Dance people call it a musical drawing. You never know beforehand what the music drawing or finger dance drawing will eventually look like.

10

The music will decide. The children will learn this at a very early age and will continue to do so the rest of their lives. For instance, if you are happy or sad, impatient or angry, you will first make your music drawing on a special wall in the house to loosen up your fingers and then make a wall painting in which you will show your feelings. If after a couple of years all the walls of a Write Dance house are covered from top to bottom, the people just cover them with some fresh terracotta coloured clay and begin all over again. Therefore, it is possible that some walls of very old houses will hide numerous paintings over each other.

The lady with the playful dog, which finally became tired and stayed with us, went on to say that you will also find Write Dance paths or Write Dance lines around the village. They are two narrow little paths of several dozens of metres long, running parallel to each other, which have been created by walking a dance, or dancing while walking. One of the two paths has been covered in white powdered chalk. The trick is to make steps with one or two feet on the white path and then to make prints on the path that has not been covered, in other words you jump from one path to the other. You could do this slowly, so that it looks more like walking or a little faster so that it looks more like dancing. There also appear to be Write Dance people who are very good at doing this with hands and feet at the same time.

As soon as such a Write Dance path or Write Dance line has been created, a three or four year old child is chosen. The Write Dance child carries a small wooden bucket with paint and with its little feet the child will walk or dance between the white prints of the big people's dancing footsteps. Every now and then the child will sprinkle a drop of paint as if it were a small petal. That is how little children learn to make dancing steps at an early age and to follow a line of movements.

If it doesn't rain or if there is no wind and the weather remains fine for a little while, you could trace the Write Dance lines on the clear path once again. Usually, a short rhyme or a short song will simply enter your head.

When the lady had finished telling her story, I looked into her eyes for quite a while. Had she told me a fairytale or is this really true? Today I still don't know...

How Write Dance evolved

I started Write Dance at the end of the eighties, not because of an educational background, but from the perspective of a graphologist. As a certified graphologist I studied hand-written applications, commissioned by companies. I also taught graphology. Graphology as a discipline is close to psychology, particularly the theory of personality.

- *The famous psychologist Klages saw the rise of modern graphology around 1900 (together with the doctor Crépieux-Jamin). Klages warned that certain characteristics in handwriting should not be thought to have set meanings. He always takes note of the handwriting in its entirety. He teaches us to judge handwriting according to its authenticity and personal movements of expression. After all, all handwriting is unique. In Write Dance I would like to make this fundamental graphological approach available to education.*

Around 1980 I met the Dutch graphologist C. Haenen-van der Hout. She ran a practice offering pedagogical support in handwriting, tutoring children with writing problems individually. Her starting point was Magdalena Heermann's therapy, but Mrs Haenen added her own touch. I, too, assisted in her practice for a while. Mrs Haenen suggested I should experiment with music.

- *Magdalena Heermann's Schreibbewegungstherapy is a form of graphotherapy. Heermann diagnosed children and teenagers with psychiatric and behavioural problems based on a disturbed personal rhythm in their handwriting. By means of hand-writing exercises on a very large board, reaching from the floor to the ceiling she wanted to restore that rhythm. In particular she focused on the alternation of tension and relaxation. She worked together with a psychiatrist in Bielefeld and saw good results. I adopted her notion of 'writing movement'. Heermann worked with a variety of looped garlands, arches and angles. I added a couple of foundation movements. Heermann worked in one-to-one relationships from a therapeutic point of view, while Write Dance is mainly intended to be used in groups. You might be able to call Write Dance preventative, rather than therapeutic, but it is particularly a very playful activity.*

In 1987 my family and I moved to Sweden, where I had the opportunity to experiment with my own ideas about writing movement to music in a number of primary schools. To my great surprise Write Dance was a great success and appreciated by children as well as teachers, which led to its publication, first in Sweden, followed by a number of other countries. I chose the name Write Dance because of the part music plays in it. Dancing is moving to music, Write Dancing is writing movements to music.

- *In today's society with all our computers and keyboards, handwriting plays a much smaller part than it used to. At the same time the attitude to children has changed. We no longer wish to force children into a straitjacket. For this reason a formal instruction of handwriting focusing on prescriptive schoolish letter shapes is no longer adequate. Therefore I suggest in Write Dance to change our starting point: shape is no longer our top priority, instead movements take over. 'Technical' writing is no longer a prerequisite before we allow an individual style to develop. From the start we can give our style a personal touch.*

Mrs Haenen has published significantly about the instruction of handwriting but she did not manage to develop her own ideas into a concrete methodology. She was more interested in expression and creativity. It is an objective I took to heart in Write Dance. By placing expression at the centre, the instruction of handwriting is presented in a wider perspective than previously. I can see a continuous line from the first scribbles to learning to form letters. In Write Dance we can monitor the entire development in a relaxed, playful way, which is not product focused. If a child is first allowed to scrimble and write draw, he or she can eventually learn to write in a very relaxed manner.

- *The relationship of scrimbling and writing is similar to that of crawling and walking. Scrimbling is the development of squiggling and scribbling and prior to the most elementary foundation movements. The foundation movements magnify the movements that lay the foundation of handwriting. The progress from scrimbling to write drawing and writing largely follows the composition of Write Dance in the Early Years and Write Dance to More Write Dance, but even in More Write Dance plenty of attention is given to write drawing and music drawing. Generally speaking we progress from movements in the air to movements on a surface, from big to small, from working with two hands to working with one hand, from movement to shape. Whenever it becomes too difficult and the hands tend to clench up, it is best to return to the elementary movements in a big way. Because only when movements are performed well, is it possible for a successful shape to develop. The write drawings consist of writing movements that may lead to recognizable shapes without them being recognized as letters. For instance, think of the cave drawings in the Stone Age and the Egyptians' hieroglyphs. When write drawing the child can allow its fantasy to flow and express its own world of experience. The letters emerge from the same movements as those which we have already applied in write drawing. The letters are immediately connected with small sound words. There will always be space for loosening up movements and write drawing by means of playing with letters and pictorial letters.*

There used to be a strong social necessity to have a uniform style of handwriting. The rise, first of typewriters, followed by word processors meant that such a need has grown smaller. Is it still necessary to learn to write by hand? Yes, just like we still need to learn to do arithmetic, even though there are calculators. And we still need to learn to walk, even though there are cars. Children often miss out when it comes to movement. Insufficient outdoor play and the inundation of signals via screens which you can't process adequately can be detrimental to our social, emotional and intellectual development in many ways. Relaxed write dancing, writing movements to music, has become a wholesome counterbalance. Handwriting is one of our most personal means of expression and the development of our handwriting cannot be separated from our general development. Write Dance is a total experience, including emotions and fantasy. And each child can do it, even children with developmental delay, because they give it their own touch from the start, which they will enhance as they are going along. Of course their intellectual development will benefit as well.

The reviewed continuum in Write Dance in the Early Years, Write Dance and More Write Dance has not developed as a series of tailor-made lessons. Its use will vary too much; in the classroom, in small groups or individually, or in mainstream education, special needs education or in practices for child physiotherapy, occupational therapy or remedial therapy. It will also depend on the teachers' familiarity with the material. The material can be chosen to fit any situation and it can be used according to its suitability to the circumstances.

Graphology and Write Dance

Handwriting is the visible reflection of expressions on a writing surface. It is the reflection of our personality. Graphology offers a closer study. In the sixty years between 1880 and 1940 graphology developed significantly:

- Klages was the first to introduce rhythm when studying handwriting and he paid particular attention to the relationship between control and spontaneity.
- Crépieux-Jamin prioritised the level of harmony.
- Heiss focused on *shape*, *space* and *movement*, and noted that good shapes could only develop if there was supple movement within a good distribution of space.
- The brain physiologist Pophal investigated the levels of tension, in which slack and loose lines are juxtaposed to stiff and tense lines, leaving elasticity and bounce in between, demonstrating the author's equilibrium.
- Pulver had an original perception of the writing surface and writing process. "When I begin to write something, immediately whatever I have written belongs to the past. Empty areas need to be filled with writing and represent the future". He did not only associate the direction 'to the right' with the future, but also with 'the other person' as we write from left to right with the intention of communicating something to the other person. Likewise Pulver also interpreted the concepts of up and down. Up stands for the sky, your head, your thoughts. Down stands for earth, feet, matter. This equals the symbolism of the cross, i.e. top and bottom, left and right.

All these graphological variables constitute the foundation of my method Write Dance. I use it practically for children, all children, regardless of their motor skills, and from a very early age. We allow the children to play and experiment with graphological features unknowingly, and initially they will do so with their whole body. *Physical awareness, a sound rhythm and smooth and effortless handwriting are our aims.*

Body awareness and its importance for psychomotor skill

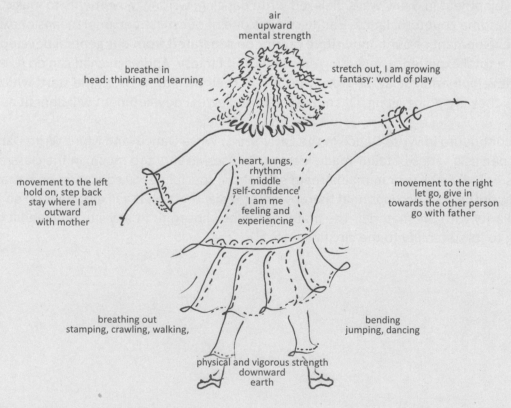

Twelve important characteristics of handwriting judged by graphologists

In graphology we make statements and find explanations by measuring, testing, comparing and combining. Each characteristic has a positive or a less positive explanation, depending on the circumstances and the surroundings and therefore is always relative.

1. At the top – upward
My head is at the top of my body
I can feel the power in my head
I breathe in and I make myself tall, I stretch and I feel happy
I want to reach, higher and higher, learn even more

2. At the bottom – downward
I am standing on my feet
I feel the wholesome strength in my feet and leg
I breathe out, I can walk and move
I collapse, I have lost interest

Between top and bottom
... are my lungs: I can breathe in and out
... are my heart and my tummy: they tell me what I feel
I like to turn around, it makes everything different.
I like jumping up and down,
to play football, to swing and to dance

3. Tall
Look how tall I am!
When I have grown up....
Tall, taller, tallest,
I like space, or turn away from it

4. Small
I am the smallest
Small is great,
but too small is really too small
... just look how tiny!

Between tall and small
My coat, my shoes are too sizes too big,
I will grow into them...
First I will make some very big movements, which is good for my body,
and then movements in the writing area around me,
and then I will do some finger sports!

5. Wide
I am taking very big steps
I will reach you in a few steps
I want to go with you
My clothes are nice and baggy

6. Tight
I am taking shorter steps
I am careful with my energy,
small steps forward
I am being careful, which makes me feel safe
Sometimes I get frightened!

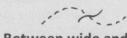

Between wide and narrow
Eyes open: day   Eyes shut; night
Ears open: hear   Ears shut: don't want to hear / listen
Open mouth: eating and speaking   Mouth shut: don't want to share
                                       – I am not going to

Open nose: everything smells wonderful!   Shut nose: I can't smell anything...
Hands: I can't (don't want to) touch you
Hands in pockets: I will stay where I am

7. Slowly

I will take it easy
I will control myself
I want to do it precisely
I can't move any faster because my body, head, fingers
can't move any faster
I hold on to shape (forced)

8. Fast

I love running
I am agile, spontaneous and also a little impulsive
When I run too fast, I trip up
I let go quickly
I can (am allowed to) be very messy

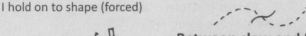

Between slow and fast, tight and loose

I am enjoying write walking
Feet: I am healthy and like physical exercise
Head: I am well built
Heart: I can laugh loudly but also cry loudly!
I am me, I want and I can!

9. Hard pressure

Look at my strength!
I am strong, I would like to be a toughy!
I can push you away, you can't push me over.
I grit my teeth, I swallow my tears

10. Light pressure

I feel and experience so much, but how do I deal with it?
Sometimes I feel as light as a feather,
it is difficult to keep up straight
I don't like it when children aren't nice
Sometimes I am very tired

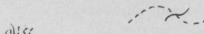

Between hard and light pressure

I love jumping, because I can feel my feet on the ground
and my head is in the air
I love twirling because everything turns around me,
but sometimes I crash on the floor!
I have forgotten what I want and can do, feel or experience, so I'll be firm!

11. Full - round

Look how many pancakes I have eaten!
I make my mouth nice and round, as well as my circles
When I am happy I dance in circles
I can make train loops, my eights can also
swing round the bend
My cat's heads are soft and round
And the waves roll over the stones and shells
The numbers 0, 3 and 8 are full and round

12. Thin - line

I don't want to eat and speak, I will keep my mouth
shut firmly shut like a line
I prefer to learn and think rather than make something
When I write my letters too thinly, they won't have
any air, they won't be able to breathe!
If I find it difficult to make round shapes, it will
give me scribbly (hand)writing

Between round and empty

I have a round/empty feeling
Sufficient lies between round and empty
I have eaten too much, my tummy is too full
I haven't eaten enough, my tummy is flat
Enough is enough!

Rhythm, your own style

In Write Dance it is all about finding a good rhythm and your own style by means of:

- Spontaneity and control

- Coordination between both sides of your brain

- Scrimbling, write drawing and writing

- Working in a big space, the smaller space around you, and on a surface

- Use of all senses

- Alternation between suppleness and firmness

- Carrying out all movements with both hands: upward, downward, to the left and to the right

- Accompanied by music, singing and humming

Music

You learn to write in the same way you learn to dance. Before you can dance according to the beat and rhythm of the music, you first need to learn the steps: forward, backward. left, right, arms up, arms down, to the side... The tune will help you make smooth movements. There is a continual alternation between the senses, motor skills and brain signals. While writing, the pen dances across the paper. This also happens when writing music notes. Writing is also about making a composition of the line patterns with straight and round shapes.
When making music drawings you are a ball of movement. By first dancing the music drawings, all the cells in your body will remember how the write dance steps are made. They create a little programme for you. After that, all you need to do is lay your programme on the surface. Writing leaves a trace, dancing leaves an impression. Dancing is all about movement, write dancing is a pattern of lines and movements, a choreography on paper. Without music you would never be able to create so many lines in your music drawing. Music is the motor that sets off *scrimbling, write drawing and writing*. Music helps you go round bends and it keeps you going. Moreover music speaks to your emotions, Write Dance helps children express themselves involving their entire being.

An etymological ('etymological': study of the meaning of words) dictionary says the following:
Rhythm is alternation in movement.
Latin: rhytmus, derived from reo which means I flow.
Greek: ruthmos which means the form of movement in melody, beat, rhythm.

Therefore rhythm can mean both *beat* and *melody*. We count or walk according to the beat or we are simply *out* of time. A clock beats a regular tick - tock. The conductor of a brass band beats the rhythm with his stick. The conductor of a symphony orchestra, however, will generally also indicate the fluid movements of the melody with or without his baton.
A melodious piece of music with round fluid movements is quite different to a piece of music with march time where count and beat go together.

And of course there are rhythms in different cultures which aim to spur on people, get them moving, make their hearts beat and make you alive. Such pulsing rhythms are also heard in all kinds of music of today. They can either stir you up or drive your hearing crazy.

In the music themes of Write Dance we will be confronted with beat as well as melody. The music may stir you up or be relaxing, have a rigid beat or 'rounded' smooth melodies. We prefer to use the latter because they appeal to the emotions.

Children and adults used to be able to write for considerable time in a very regular fashion. Writing was as important as arithmetic and English. The teacher's stick would beat time and pace: thin strokes up, thick strokes down. Everybody would be writing at the same time in the very strict pattern of movements. All handwriting was quite similar. This has changed. Children and adults write how they feel they should or *quite contrary* to the way they feel they should. And the latter is increasingly common today. You might call it irregular or non-rhythmic handwriting, which manifests itself with jumps and starts, it is tense or falls apart and it features incoherence. Therefore it stands to reason that we teach children from an early age to manage good and positive rhythms and melodies in which they can express themselves, either dancing with their whole body or on flat surfaces. In Write Dance we have replaced the teacher's stick with the CD player which produces a variety of rhythms and moods. That is how a sound rhythm can be acquired. Writing is given a new chance to develop. Letters and joins begin to belong together, they create little families, sentences become small units and written pieces become 'presentable'. They represent totality, harmony. They are clear, legible and pleasing to look at.

In Write Dance we teach the children to sense their *own swing* in such a way that it feels entirely natural, it comes naturally, it makes you feel good. The child enjoys the smooth flow of dance and writing (symbols) without having to use too much energy. The stream is like a river on which you might experience anything.

We could compare the development of fine motor skills to learning to play music instruments, such as a piano or flute. The Japanese Suzuki developed a method in the seventies for very young violinists and pianists so that they could immediately play a tune. He would choose generally known melodies such as 'Twinkle twinkle little star...' or 'Frère Jacques'. He would immediately offer such a melody in different rhythms. The foundation of his method was therefore *learning to manage joins and entities*, not unconnected notes or technical details. Suzuki proved the impact of his method by forming a string orchestra of more than a hundred children within three months. Write Dance chooses a similar starting point: it is not necessary to start with technical fine motor skills exercises but you can learn to express yourself immediately from an early age either in the air, on a board or on paper. When you are ready to write letters, you can immediately connect them the way you feel it is right, in groups of two, three or four.

We can prevent tension by occasionally raising our wrists slightly above the surface. We call it *low doodling.* It is also possible to create *high doodling*, by raising our arm(s) high in the air, by relaxing our shoulders and arms completely. We will see a good pianist do the same. He will take time to let the music penetrate completely and relax his hand without losing touch with his playing. Similarly the Write Dancer does not lose touch with the pattern of lines while doodling.

Foundation movements and the nine music themes *Volcano to Mandala*

Writing is a process full of complexity, where circle dissections and straight lines attract and reject each other. If a good foundation has not been laid in which movements are distinguished and combined, it could give rise to confusion which results not only in writing problems but also in reading problems. All foundation movements can be made along horizontal, vertical or diagonal lines or in circles. The first nine music themes Volcano to Mandala form a comprehensive unit in which all foundation movements in the air and on the surface are combined with music.

1 *Volcano*

2 *Walk / Krongelidong*

3 *Circles and Eights*

4 *Robot*

5 *Train*

6 *The Tree*

7 *The Sea / Silver Wings*

8 *Cats / Ocean Waves*

The circle

9 *Mandala / Flower Garlands*

1. The circle is split in two by means of a horizontal or a vertical line. Hollow and round shapes emerge.

2. They attract each other and create a new harmonious circle or they reject each other when moved, and create duality and problems.

Harmony gives movement and smooth waves.

3. Loops upward emerge from the rotating movement to the left and a move to the right in the writing direction.

4. Loops downward emerge from rotating movements to the right and moves to the right.

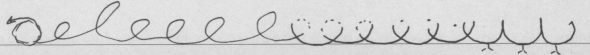

The garland

The garland is a string of upward loops or a chain if we leave the loops out.
It bears an element of relaxation and openness. Every part is an open dish, a cup or a boat.

Symbolic

My dish is open, something may fall into it
I can receive, share and empathise
I am open to everything around me...
I can thread a necklace, feminine
She rocks me to sleep

The arch

The arch is a garland with loops downward or curves if we leave out the loops.
It bears an element of tension and privacy. Every part is an arch.

Symbolic:

I have turned the dish over, I am protecting what lies underneath
I protect myself from signals from the outside
I want to stay in the centre, and concentrate
I can stand under an arch, and I will feel safe
I can be independent, build an arch, masculine

Straight, flat line   *horizontal*

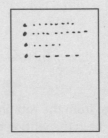

The flat line moves from side to side   *The ground, the earth*

Left = past
If I begin to write to the left of the surface
and then move to the right, then the left
will immediately become the past!

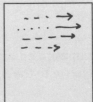

Right = future
If I move my writing instrument to the right,
I will still have to complete the rest of the line.
I am going to do so.

Straight, upright line *vertical*

The upright line moves up and down *Earth and sky*

I'll begin to write at the top. Shortly after
the top will be the past. In the empty area
below I will make some writing movements
write drawing or writing.

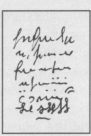

Upward and downward

I breathe in, the movement goes up
I stretch my back, I stretch myself

I breathe out, the movement goes down again
I bend my back, I bend down

Square and triangle

A square develops by combining
horizontal and vertical lines
When they move, it creates an upright cross

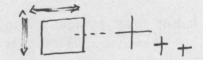

A triangle is created by three diagonal lines
When the lines move it creates a diagonal cross

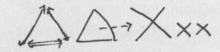

Movement and shape

Movements … condense … into set shapes … and dissolve again into movements …

Movements … proceed … to be unconnected … and reconnected …

The nine foundation themes from the child's perspective

1. Volcano *Rumbling lines, slanting lines, dots, loop and dashes*

    This is my mountain
    Downward: my feet are firmly on the ground
    O dear, the earth is rumbling under my feet!
    Upward: I dare to let everything go, I am jumping up in the air!

2. Walk / Krongelidong *Make krongelidongs*

    I am just walking around,
    My body and writing are supple and sound
    I am dreaming, fantasising and learning. Life is but a dream!

3. Circles and Eights *Turn around, contrasts*
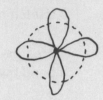

    I am turning, drawing and writing in circles, I can draw circles
    Lying eights from side to side Rockaby Baby, I will rock with you
    Upright eights *up and down*, wake up,
    The night has passed, it is half past seven!
    Eight of clubs *I get up and go back to bed*, get up, go to sleep.

4. Robot *Sharp, straight and angular*

    I am as strong as a robot, as a castle, as an iceberg.
    I like counting, sums and working and I can do it on my own

5. Train *I will let my loops go*

    My life at (school) is rolling along fine
    My letters are rolling out of the train

6. The Tree *Seeds and plants, fragile lines up, the trunk*

    I am growing, moving and feeling
    The trunk: straight lines down, here is my tree!
    Branches: sharp lines up, I am growing…
    Leaves: loops around and I am blossoming!

7. The Sea / Silver Wings *Waves*

    On the waves of the sea I sway along
    A bit of wind is good for every child
    In the storm I almost break

8. Cats / Ocean Waves *Three quarter circles*

    From side to side and a little bit more
    From my neck to my nose and back...
    and then I arch my back like a cat
    Cats at sea, high waves, oh dear!

9. Mandala *Straight and round in a circle*
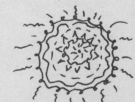

    I am a flower, I am a sun, I am a star and come from afar
      Dancing and writing will be here forever!

An overview of the Write Dance Method

In the Write Dance method the nine foundation themes *Volcano to Mandala* are central. Although the drawings of the songs in Write Dance in the Early Years are simplified versions, they have been presented in a unique manner, with their own stories and music. In this book *Write Dance* you will also find that there are variations of the foundation themes in the songs and in the variation themes *Rocket to Rosette*.

Write Dance in the Early Years	Write Dance		
Foundation theme **Home** Variation theme **Fun Fair**	Foundation theme	*Song*	Variation theme
Singing and scrimbling Song drawing	*Music drawing*	*Singing and write drawing*	*Music drawing*
1 **Sandy Hill** **Watermill**	**Volcano** *Warming up, dynamic tension, liberation*	**Volcano song** Holca Volca...	**Rockett** *Fire, launch, cockpit, earth, descent*
2 **Kringeli-krangeli** **Dinky Car**	**Walk /** **Krongelidong** *Relaxation and rest, orientation, fantasy*	**Krongeli animals-song** We are the Krongeli animals	**Space-walk** *Floating, discovering, noises and planets*
3 **Pancakes** **Merry-go-round**	**Circles and Eights** *Round movements, crossing, melody*	**Round-and-round-song** Just look what I have found...	**Flowers and Ladybirds** *Special flower, insects*
4 **The Staircase** **The Procession**	**Robot** *Straight movements, beat and structure*	**Robot-song** Hinki tinki...	**Robot-procession** *Robots, squeaks, crackles, lights and lids*
5 **The Toy Train** **Air Train**	**Train** *Looped arcades and garlands, from slow to fast*	**Train song** Choo choo...	**Cowboys and Indians** *Train, fast train, Indians and cowboys*
6 **Tickle leaves** **Fairy Light Tree**	**The Tree** *Stroke up and stroke down, loops around*	**The Tree Song** Hold tight, hold tight...	**Rain Forest** *Birds and monkeys*
7 **Little Water Shute** **Big Water Shute**	**The Sea / Silver Wings** *Wavy movements, From lapping to stormy*	**See-song** Take me with you...	**The River /** **Pleasure boat** *Waves, Write Dance drawing*
8 **The Rainbow** **The Gateway**	**Cats / Ocean waves** *Three quarter circles, from side to side and joined*	**Cats-song** Miaow, miaow...	**Cats, Guinea Pigs and Fish** *High jumps and long jumps, maze and fish*
9 Little Sun **Dear Sun, Dear Moon**	**Mandala** *Repeat of the eight foundation themes in rings round a central point*	**Mandala-song** I am a star...	**Rosette** *Repeat of the variation themes*
10 straight, bent, cross, happy, angry			

Write Dance	More Write Dance
Psychomotor objective	**Learning to write**
Foundation theme and Variation theme	*Write Drawing, Sound Words, Pictorial Letters, six Music drawings*

	Psychomotor objective	Learning to write
1	*Volcano: Earth - ground, Sky - freedom, Shaking - loosening, Thunder and Lightning - tension and relaxation, Rain - rhythm and motor challenge.* *Rocket: Fire - shake loose, Cockpit - space / floating, Planet Earth - recognition and emotion, Landing - coming home*	*Strokes down, strokes up, loops, waves, dots, dashes*
2	*Whether we are walking on earth or in space, we will experience a sense of adventure and freedom. Fantasy will play a lively part. We will meet krongelidong-animals; associations with music and sounds will inspire us.*	*Smooth movements in all directions in preparation of joined-up handwriting*
3	*The circle and smooth lines are the foundations in order to express write dance-flowers. The horizontal, vertical and eight-leaf clover belong together and are developed in the variation theme. We patter and draw insects in a straight line or all over.*	*The circle as a foundation. We discover letters in the eight-leaf clover*
4	*Robots make straight and angular movements and they are a good contrast to the previous theme. Many Robots together create a lot of noise, crackles and squeaks. We make up an entire robot-family.*	*The straight line and angle as a foundation encourages firm handwriting. Basic structure of capital letters*
5	*The train speeds through the Wild West and is stopped by the Indians. Their rhythm inspires an Indian dance and feathers and a lot of dashes. The cowboys return the two cows and it all ends well!*	*An alternation of looped arches and garlands. Important for upper and lower loops. Managing contrasts. Alternating rhythm*
6	*Many trees make a forest or rain forest. We experience an exciting adventure where animal noises scare us. We make a creative drawing and the music may be repeated infinitely. This can be combined with 'Flowers and Ladybirds'.*	*Using light pressure upward, pressure downward. Trunk and firmness, loops and looseness. Drawing and write drawing go together*
7	*We sail on a calm sea or river and make small waves. The wind rises and the waves become higher and higher, and a storm develops! The boats go up and down but the Pleasure Boat remains calm.*	*The arch and the garland-boat merge in waves without any problems. Alternation of beats*
8	*Cats, guinea pigs and fish are the stars of the Olympic Games for Pets. Above and on the surface the dogs play football, the cats jump high and far, but the fish don't bat an eyelid...!*	*Three quarter curves joined up are the foundations of the letters a c d g. Game and playfulness. The foundation of your own style and rhythmic handwriting*
9	*The Mandala and Rosette will repeat all the music for us in shortened versions. We make a sun, a star, a church window, a flower garland or a write drawing dance. Straight and round shapes and all their variations alternate.*	*Repeats in shortened versions of the music pieces. Listening, expressing and representing. A foundation of a supple, smooth and resilient handwriting*

In scrimbling and write drawing to music foundation movements are practised in a variety of combinations, which invariably leads to learning to write.

The writing movements necessary for writing no longer present fundamental problems. It also feels very natural to join the letters from the start.

In More Write Dance the letters are discussed alphabetically, always combined with a writing sheet and a page 'Playing with the letter'. These writing sheets can be used in any order of letters as required.

When sound writing, the letters are joined up immediately into small 'sound words' in which vowels and consonants continue to alternate. The sound words easily lead on to fantasy sentences and stories. Pictorial letters activate the pupil's fantasy.

The forerunner of the writing sheet in More Write Dance — see copy sheets, available to print from the SAGE website www.uk.sagepub.com/writeDance2

Letters will not be discussed until More Write Dance. But anyone who wishes to begin with letters in Write Dance can use a very simple writing sheet as follows.

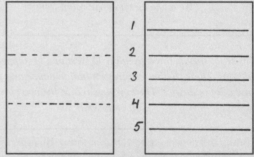

We divide the sheet into five lines by first
folding the sheet into three parts
Then we fold back each area once.
We can also make a copy of it.

We trace the first line from side to side with the forefinger of the assisting hand and look for the centre while singing a tune "Where is the centre, where is the centre, put a dot in it".

We will repeat this searching for the centre twice which will give us 5 dots.

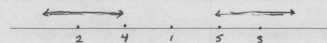

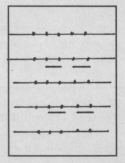

Then we draw a line under dots 2 and 3 on
the second line and a line under dots 4 and 5 on the 4th line.
On the table top we can follow the same procedure
by drawing lines of chalk.

A few suggestions for foundation exercises on five dots

On this writing sheet enough space remains to make decorations all around just like we do in the story drawing. When a young child becomes accustomed to this without too much strained effort, joining letters will not present too many problems as we will learn in More Write Dance, and using he 9 dot writing sheet.

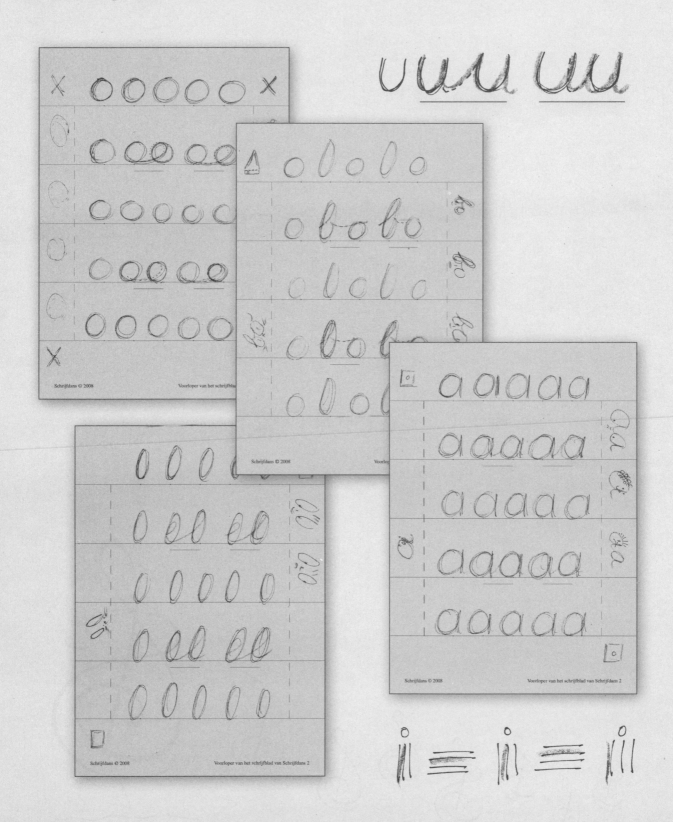

Materials and practical applications

A big room

PE hall, free play room, school yard

All the movements in music themes are always practised first with your whole body in a big room.

Classroom, therapy room

1. The movements are first practised using your whole body while standing behind tables.

2. Followed by sitting down, while your torso continues to move along smoothly!

3. Then we make our fingers dance, which is 'finger dancing' in preparation of write drawing.

4. After finger dancing we will use write drawing material which then becomes appropriate

- *Finger dancing* This is a method which prepares fingers for write drawing. Lines in chalk or pencil drawn too soon might lead to a fear of failure, which is exactly what Write Dance aims to prevent. Finger dancing is something we will also do afterwards to try and experience the movements once again... We could also use finger dancing to repeat a music drawing which we have already practised. We will do this directly on the table top without any materials, ideally one or two minutes every day in the air, at or on the tables, instead of once a fortnight for half an hour to an hour.

Materials to be used in a big room

All kinds of objects

- *Boxes, hoops*   We walk or dance among them

- *A long piece of rope*   It shows the direction for walking or dancing,
                                            which could also be shown in chalk on the floor

- *Ribbons, scarves, etc.*   They clearly show the movements and add colour to the room.
                                            The scarves may also be used as markings to
                                            replace the rope or line of chalk.

Write drawing-surfaces   vertical and horizontal

In Write Dance we work on board and paper, on a wet or a dry surface, on walls and doors, on the floor and on the table top. Alternating between vertical and horizontal surfaces is good practice for the whole body, hands, eyes and ears.

Big boards on the wall of the PE hall

We use MDF boards of 122 x 61 cm. The thickness should be about 4 to 6 mm. They are available in any DIY store.

Cover the board on one side with blackboard paint in the required colour and attach it firmly to the wall. If there is enough room, attach two or three big boards beside each other. Each one can accommodate two children for write drawing.

Doors

If there isn't enough wall space we could cover one or two doors of the sports hall with blackboard paint. Even large sheets of paper can be taped to doors or windows.

Blackboard paint

This is available in paint stores in the colours black, green, bright red or bright blue. Nowadays you can also have blackboard paint mixed in any required colour. Pastel shades are pleasing to the eyes. One or two layers of paint applied with a roller should be sufficient. The paint dries quickly..

Sponges, cloths, washing flannel mittens

We use ordinary household sponges. Each child working on the big wall board will need two halves of a big sponge. They will need them not only to clean, but they can also use the tip to do some '*sponge dancing*' in preparation of, or as an alternative to write drawing in chalk.

Collect plenty of plastic containers for the slightly dampened sponges. And you will need jay cloths and wash mitts to dry the boards. If you cannot find any wash mitts in e.g. supermarkets you can easily make them yourself from washing flannels.

Finger dancing on the blackboard

With our fingers we dance in the damp lines until the latter have dried. This will improve our tactile sense and it is possible to create new variations over and on top of the dry lines.

Blackboard chalk

Plain white or coloured blackboard chalk is quite suitable for the big board or the table board. The more expensive anti-dust chalk is advisable for use in a therapy room. Break the pieces of chalk in halves so that they can be picked up from above to avoid the hammer grip. The hammer grip keeps wrists stiff. New, long pieces of chalk tend to break easily; they cause disappointment and hinder a smooth movement.
Only use pavement chalk outside because it creates too much dust on the blackboard.

The Write Dance table

- *DIY* The Write Dance table is a round table covered in blackboard paint with a diameter of about 140 cm. There is a hole in the centre of about 60 cm. The table is divided in two halves, kept together with hooks and slides. Five detachable legs have been screwed into each half. The table can be used in various different ways.
  - One child stands in the centre. Just as in circle games the focus will be on the child in the centre. This can be fun and result in teamwork with the pupils who are write dancing around the child. Write drawing all around helps the development of orientation.
  - The two halves can also be used separately by placing them upright. The children will sit with their legs in the hole and can write draw in semi-circular arches.
  - The two halves can also be used when playing ball games.

- *Recycled table* This is a simplified version of the Write Dance table. It could be a round table or alternatively an oval shaped table with four legs. Saw a hole in it with the jigsaw, saw the legs to size if necessary and paint the surface in blackboard paint. If there is enough space, this table would remain permanently in the communal area.

- *Coffee table* This can be bought in charity shops for little money and they are available in all kinds of sizes. Their height will be around 47 cm which is the ideal height for children aged 4-6. Cover them in blackboard paint and that is all you need to do. Some tables will have a magazine shelf, which is useful to have containers with sponges and chalk readily available.

The write dance area

Find a suitable place for an oblong table covered in blackboard paint and have a CD player handy which can be managed by a pupil. Don't forget to provide a (table) board on the wall in order to be able to work on a vertical surface, including materials for write drawing. When the table is dry we could also simply put down some sheets of paper to work on. It means that pupils can work in the write dance area at any time of day by themselves or in pairs.

In case you have a smartboard in the classroom and you cannot work on it with both hands simultaneously, nor place different colours over each other, please hang a (table) board beside.

Music drawings and write drawings on dry and wet surfaces

Table board

We will have an MDF board of 122 x 61 cm and a thickness of 4 to 6 mm cut into three equal parts so we are able to work individually on the table board. The board fits a school desk exactly. An uncut board is very suitable for working in pairs. It is laid across three desks. Corners may be rounded. The boards are painted in the required colour *on both sides*. To prevent slipping we should put anti-slip mats underneath. Store the boards in the same place, for example close to the write dance area. The pupils can use the boards to make music drawings, write drawing and other activities, such as arithmetic, drawing, games...

Around 12 table boards will need to be made for a group of approximately 25 children and leave one MDF board uncut to be used by pairs.

For 'sponge dancing' and cleaning the table board you will need to cut the big sponge into 6-8 pieces. You can make attractive prints with the small squares. You could also squeeze them firmly so that some water drips on the board. We will play in the wet and dry areas. You can continue to finger dance on a wet table board until the surface is completely dry.

Sand

Sand is one of the natural products in which people used to make figures with sticks or fingers in prehistoric times. In Write-Dance we will continue this custom.

Many kinds of 'therapeutic sand' are available, but it is best to buy ordinary play sand. If it contains fine pieces of shell, they will stimulate our tactile sense.
Sprinkle a thin layer in a garden tray, a tea tray or in the lid of a big shoebox; you could put a (table)cloth or a sheet underneath to cover the entire table so any sand that falls over the edge can be shaken off easily.

Slippery paint and shaving foam

Slippery paint is easy to make. Detergent, shower gel, shampoo, liquid soap, preferably anti allergenic or ordinary paste are the main ingredients of slippery paint.

Pour or pump some soap from a bottle directly onto the table surface. A plastic surface is suitable too, but as we clean everything to music after we have finished, working on a plastic surface on ordinary school desks is not really necessary. We will drop some poster paint into the smooth soapy surface, or we will sprinkle some coloured powder and off we go.
The most beautiful line and colour patterns will develop while finger dancing and later we will make prints of them. Occasionally spray a little water on the coloured soapy area from a plant or a window spray. If the soap dries, the movements will not be as smooth. Generous spraying will give us a foaming surface which is a fun experience too.
Of course there are always children who will be afraid of a surface in which their fingers slip. A simple solution is a small piece of sponge attached to a clothes peg. It means that it is not their fingers that will slip in the paint.

You can draw beautiful thin tracks in the slippy surface with a bamboo stick, cotton tips or the back of a clothes peg or with miniature cars. The print will be even more interesting.

Shaving foam Don't spray the foam in a heap but into a long thin line and dampen it here and there with a bit of water. It means that it won't stick to your fingers as much and we can draw lines and figures in it at once. You can also add a drop of paint to the shaving foam.

Print

It is possible to make a print from slippery paint after write drawing just like we did after scrimbling in Write Dance in the Early Years. A sheet of A3 paper is ideal.

The amount of slippy material will determine the sharpness of the lines in the print.
You can make various prints of one and the same wet surface, because the line and colour structures will always be a surprise. Prints could dry on a washing line or simply on the floor and the beautiful artwork can be used for all kinds of purposes. When it has dried completely, we will give the children crayons and coloured pencils to let their imagination go. Real-life or imaginary figures are cut out and could be stuck on boxes. Prints on wrapping paper will make presents more attractive and original for father's day and mother's day.

Wash mitts

After making a print we clean the surface again. We use washing flannel mittens to do this, one on each hand. That is how we work when cleaning with both hands. When one side of the mitt has been used, we turn it over to use the upper side. The mittens needn't be washed after each use. We hang them from a washing line in the classroom or peg them to a clothes horse. The shaving foam or liquid soap will spread a pleasant odour through the room.

Don't forget to do some 'dry' finger dancing during the week, directly on the table. If you do this for two minutes every day it will reinforce the brain programme.

Aprons

You will generally find aprons of some kind in most classrooms and therapy areas. If this is not the case, tear a sheet or piece of material into squares of about 50 x 50 cm and cut a hole for the head.

Masks

In Write Dance we often work with our eyes shut. It brings you closer to having it at your 'finger tips' or as we say in write dance terms 'finger dance sensitivity'. Sometimes eyes can be awkward critics. "Just look how awful, I am not doing it well, my neighbour / my sibling can do it much better... My mother says..."
If you don't look, everything is right, nothing is wrong, you have an 'excuse' to do it 'differently' because you write with your heart, which tells you what is really happening to the feelings inside you.
Your hands and fingers pass on the signals. When we are working with our entire body we can shut our eyes too. We do so to allow our senses to speak, but it is also a good exercise in balance.

When you close your eyes it is easier to relax. If you can't, it means there is still a large amount of insecurity and fear in your mind which will have a negative affect on your functioning. Once the writing has become totally automated and runs smoothly, a child or adult can also make notes at night without switching on the light.

We can use tea towels, cloths and shawls, but it is fun making your own masks and they can be made very colourful.

Make a mask out of strong paper or cardboard.
A piece of elastic will complete it! Now each pupil can decorate their own mask as they wish. A piece of material glued to the back will give it additional firmness.

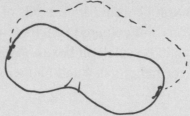

How to store Write Dance material

A hammock in three parts like a fishing net is useful for sponges that need to dry and to store trays, chalk, scarves etc. Initially ask the children to make a music drawing on a strong piece of cardboard. If you fold it and put a piece of elastic round it, it will be a folder for all future music drawings and other kinds of drawings...

Paper in all kinds of shapes and sizes

Write Dance requires a lot of paper. Many printers are happy to give away remnants, but very often you can ask parents who may be able to acquire paper at work or in the office. The paper should not be too smooth because the crayons will slip. Rolls of wallpaper are very welcome but do use rolls without relief. Of course 'school paper' can be used too. A pack of A3 sheets is usually available in school and in the therapy room. They are, however, on the small side for music drawings.

Masking tape and Blu-Tack

Each piece of paper needs to be attached firmly as we will be making the music drawings with both hands to encourage a balance between both hands and halves of the brain. We simply use masking tape or buddies. Each child is given a piece of tape of about 20 cm, tears it into four pieces and firmly attaches the paper in the corners. We could also use Blu-Tack, although it is more expensive. To prevent the Blu-Tack from disappearing quickly we will have trays with a photo or picture on it for each child. Each child will put back their Blu-Tack where it belongs.

We can use both front and back of the paper on which we make the music drawing. Any streaks of crayon on the table can be cleaned very quickly with some shaving foam, water from the spray and the wash mitts and of course to music!

In order to spend a little less time on Write Dance preparations it might be a good idea to have the Write Dance lesson after outdoor play. You can always find some children who are happy to fasten the sheets of paper in preparation.

Once we are on our way with Write Dance, we could place another sheet of A3 paper or a sheet of A4 under the big sheet for further exercises and to work from big size to small size. Another method is to take some Blu-Tack and attach a second sheet to the big sheet with the music drawing.

Crayons

In many respects coarse crayons are preferable to thin ones. Short and used stumps are gripped from above which prevents the wrists being held in the (hammer)grip position. Advice: do not hesitate to break new crayons in two.

Coloured pencils

They are suitable when using the writing hand to apply some details after the music drawing has been completed. Felt tips will quickly spoil the creative pattern of lines.
Pupils with sound fine motor skills might find write drawing with two coloured pencils a fun challenge but it is generally not advisable.

Occupational therapy materials

These materials of any kind can be used for Write Dance.
A *handy tip*: buy a plastic toolbox with a lid, preferably in a big size. It is possible to store all kinds of chalks and crayons, spinning tops, squeezy balls and feel balls in the compartments. It means that everything is ready at hand. Using different materials for write drawing is extremely helpful to the development of fine motor skills.

The nine songs

We can use the songs in the same way as the music drawings. But the songs also lend themselves to a small or a big performance.

In the classroom

Two or three 'movement children' perform movements in the air on either side of the big board. Two 'board children' write draw on the big board. We will use chalk, sponges, chamois sponges or cloths but also fingers to write draw. As described in the text the children occasionally also make movements in the air. The write dance material is held in their hands. Of course dancing and karaoke in the classroom would make a nice change.

A mini performance

After some rehearsal it is possible to perform three or four songs consecutively and we will create a short musical performance with rags, ribbons, scarves, flowers and face paints which can be watched by other year groups and of course by the parents.
If there are no boards available on the walls of the PE hall or in the common room, the write dance children could also sit on the floor on a small mat to protect their knees. They use rolls of wallpaper, big sheets of paper, table boards or possibly simply slippery paint on the floor! We could also form a group of 'print and clean children'...

In the corridors or elsewhere in the building it is also possible to view music drawings made by other groups. The young children can perform a couple of rhymes. It's fun when we turn it into a Write Dance day because write dancing can also be done in the play yard by several groups simultaneously.

And... why shouldn't we make a programme booklet?

Costumes and props

1. Volcano song	*Orange and yellow crepe paper ribbons or scarves to hold and pinned to orange t-shirts*
2. Krongeli animal-song	*Two children under a sheet with eyes, ears, nose and legs painted on it*
3. Round-and-round-song	*Wooden spoon and a pot*
4. Robot-song	*Cardboard box on their heads, covered in aluminium, and tins or similar items held in their hands*
5. Train song	*A picture of a train painted on cardboard and stuck to a stick. Or a big sheet of painted cardboard which can be held by several children and carried along*
6. Tree song	*Green and brown crepe paper ribbons and a ring of leaves on their heads*
7. Sea song	*A piece of blue or purple voile of at least 3 meters is wafted up and down. Some pupils swim under it and others fly round the sea like birds*
8. Cat song	*Face paint or cat masks. Tails!*
9. Mandala song	*Flower garlands on your head and round your neck, crepe paper ribbons or scarves and anything we can think of!*

The nine variation themes

The variation themes are an extension of the foundation themes. The theme topic, but also the movements in the air and write drawing have remained the same.

We can deal with music drawings, songs and variation themes in all kinds of ways.
First we could practise the nine music drawings, then the songs, then the variation themes...
Alternatively we could first practise the foundation theme, followed immediately by the variation theme. This may also be done in groups of three. Each assistant can plan it their own way.

Foundation drawing: Cats

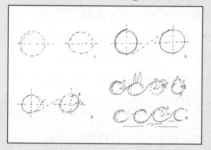

Story drawing: Cats

Foundation drawing   Story drawing   Practice on lines

Music drawings, songs and variation themes are first practiced together in class. We use the foundation drawings and story drawings, to be found as copy sheets at the back of this book, for individual work and to reinforce movements and for them to be absorbed in their world of experience. All the foundation and story drawings can be laminated and kept in a folder together, e.g. in the Write Dance area.

The foundation drawing   see copy sheets, available to print from the SAGE website www.uk.sagepub.com/writeDance2
The elementary foundation movements of the music drawing are essential to the foundation drawing. The pupils remember 'how to do it' and can repeat the write drawing independently. The copy sheets should not be 'traced'.

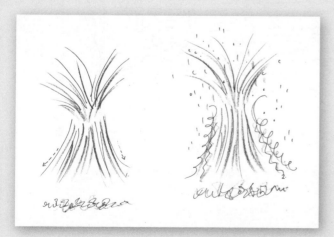

On the board or on big sheets of paper

The story drawing   see copy sheets, available to print from the SAGE website
www.uk.sagepub.com/writeDance2

The story drawing shows images in write dance style from the story or gives examples taken from the music theme. The story drawing is a source of inspiration for the children, so that they can make their own write drawings in which movement is particularly important, as well as repeated consolidation in different colours. Of course we should not forget to sing, hum and doodle at high and low level (raise your hand).
It is up to the assistant to encourage children to move freely and to use their fantasy. In this way it is possible to prevent frenetic tracing.

> *Decorative border* Each story drawing comes with a decorative border with dots. This decorative border will prepare them for write drawing on lines. The dots are there to help the children get used to spatial division. The paper can be rotated a quarter each time, so that we can make a continuous decorative border. Alternatively decorations can be made in parallel at the top and at the bottom, and to the left and to the right.

> Initially the teacher will make suggestions for decorations on the big board. Of course combinations of figures *and potential letters* are possible too. With a little experience the children will be able to decorate their own borders.

The Sea / Silver Wings

On big sheets or A3 paper

The exercises on lines   see copy sheets, available to print from the SAGE website www.uk.sagepub.com/writeDance2. They belong to the variation themes.

Each variation theme is accompanied by a lined A4 sheet. The distance between the lines is 3½ cm which is equal to the distance if we fold an A4 sheet into eight writing areas. Each line begins with an example which is continued by the children in their own style. It will then be possible to start write drawing over the example.

The teacher may also decide to start with empty lines and to show the examples or their own variations on the big board. It is not absolutely necessary to work on the lines, but the lines and any dots will offer a kind of structure. The movements are free but need some degree of control, just like a border in a garden which you can fill with plants and flowers any way you like, while remaining within the parameters of the border. Write drawing on or between lines·can be accompanied by singing or humming.

Once again we will consolidate the exercises two or three times in colour and we will write walk over the previous lines with our forefingers or coloured pencils, not precisely but smoothly and fluidly in our own style.

Write Dance © 2008   Exercise on lines 1 Rocket

Always begin on A3 paper, followed by A4 paper

39

A short Write Dance self-assessment

This little Write Dance test is meant for teacher as well as pupil. *'What did I find difficult at first and look how easy I find it now!'*

Ideally this test should be repeated three or four times during the school year, at least once before start to use Write Dance.

In general we will notice that the second and third test show more relaxed movements and that the reversal of loops runs quite smoothly. Angles have become firmer and the lines have been organised in a better way.

Method

1   Fold a sheet of A4 paper into eight writing areas. The seven lines now show a distance of approximately 3.5 cm between them. Trace them with a ruler, number the areas from 1 to 8, so that there can't be any mistakes, and make copies.

2   The assistant, back turned to the group or to the pupil, demonstrates all kinds of movements in the air. The writing movements can be done on the line or in the writing area. The pupil may choose.

3   Avoid giving too many directions. *'It doesn't matter how you do it, it is fine'*. It will give us a much more reliable picture.

1. Draw a long line

2. Draw five circles in a line

3. Draw another five circles following each other..., but now allow your pencil to trace the circle a couple of times

4. Draw a line of loops pointing upward

5. Make a line of loops pointing downward

6. We will draw a line of angles

7. Now we are going to draw eights, five in a line

8. Now choose the one you liked best. Of course you could create something yourself.

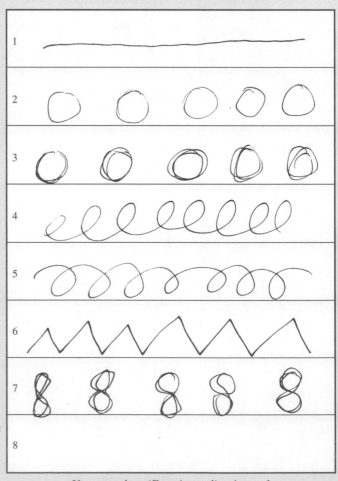

Use copy sheet 'Exercise on lines' page 1

Interpretation by graphologists

> *Weak, thin and disorganised line control:* not ready to write yet, not enough interest in the writing process. The child's emotions and fine motor skills are still developing.

> *Bold, thick lines with heavy pressure and forced writing:* good will-power but over-compensation with regard to fine motor skills.

> Now we will itemise a couple of more specific interpretations, but do be careful not to draw conclusions too quickly.

1. *The structure of the line* and its length indicate the level of vitality and purpose-mindedness. Are they spontaneous or maybe careful and precise?

2. *It is common to see circles* close together on the left. They have chosen for security. The unknown is still too remote. The more space between the circles, the more self-confidence and independence. The desire to achieve shapes is normal: a circle needs to be nice and round, but not all children can do this initially. They learn gradually

3. *Messy circles* over each other are common at first. The more their motor skills develop, the more harmonious their socio-emotional contacts. Forced attempts point to impotence or the suppression of emotional experiences.

4. *Looped garland*; relaxed and supple drawing indicates good fine motor skills and openness to others and their surroundings. Reversals and distortions tend to be common at first, thumb - forefinger motor skills and brain signals 'need to get used to each other'.

5. *Reversing the order of upward first and downward next* can be rather difficult initially. Managing opposites is not as easy yet for hand-eye-coordination. Arcade loops tend to feel more natural than garlands to most children. Their motor skills find it easier too.

6. *The angles* alternate directions; slanting upward and slanting downward, which will involve an act of will each time. The quicker the angles change into weakness, the lower the stamina. The same rule applies here: forced writing reflects a desire to achieve but with a rapid loss of energy.

7. *'Developing circles into eights'* will not be easy at first. You will learn that in Write Dance too. If they continue to take on all kinds of strange shapes, additional attention to coarse and fine motor skills will still be required.

8. *Which movement is a challenge to the child?* Will they choose the easy way or are they having fun? Fantasies always indicate liveliness.

Points to remember when making music drawings

1 **Big movements:**
In open areas such as the hall, the classroom, the school yard, nature…
always start slowly and without music.

2 **Write drawing:**
If necessary prepare with sensory-motor materials.

3 **Before you do the music drawing:**
Do some finger dancing directly on the paper: it is impossible to make
mistakes.

4 **While doing the music drawing:**

- The body needs to keep moving as fluidly as possible. Every now and
  again your feet are allowed to join as well.

- Now and then do some doodling.
  Doodling high: raise your arms and continue movements in the air to
  experience a sense of freedom.
  Doodling low: occasionally raise your hands a couple of inches above
  the sheet of paper to relax your wrists and to continue movements over
  the surface.

- Every now and then pull down the mask or close your eyes.

5 **After doing the drawing:**
Do some finger dancing to sense 'what you have
been doing'.

Somewhere not far from here, there is a small village which has hardly been visited by anyone. It is the village of the Write Dance people at the foot of the big Volcano. The people really love their environment, nature, the river, animals, singing and dancing. Everything they want to tell you, they draw and paint on the walls of their houses.

It is a sunny autumn day. The women are doing their washing in the river and the children are playing in the cool water. Then suddenly the mountain begins to shake and a big wave develops in the river and floods the banks. The Write Dance women and children are frightened when they look at the volcano and see smoke emerging. It is about to erupt, 'Quickly we must leave'.

At a safe distance they see how the fire is throwing up stones and lava hundreds of metres into the air. 'Bang, bang, bang'. And now it is beginning to thunder and lightning strikes too. The Write Dance people continue to flee further away. After four days it begins to rain gently but the people cannot return to their village, the Volcano has destroyed and burnt everything.

Warming up, dynamic tension, freedom

- The acceleration you experience while swinging on a standard swing is exciting. It gives you a sense of joy. This is what we also experience in the Volcano accelerations. You are on your way to discover and experience your own style.

- The Volcano gives you a feeling of well-being.

- Don't forget to bend your knees to find a good cadence. Your whole body is supposed to join in.

- The music will point in the right direction.

- Repetition assists a natural process.

- The big area around us is *our living quarter*; the area where we stand behind our desks is our *write dance movement space*.

- It gives us a chance to 'release' and to 'cast away' our restrained emotions.

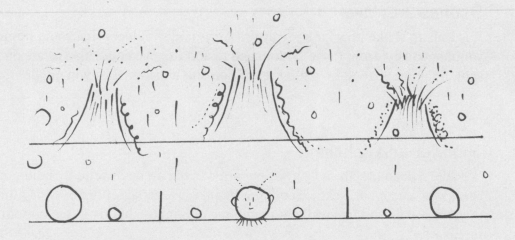

Number 1 *The stones become zeros*
The rain is expressed in dashes in preparation of number one

Movements in the air

The mountain*

We stand dispersed or in a circle and hear the rumbles rise up from the earth. Relaxed, and bending over deeply we stamp our feet, while our arms and wrists automatically shake along.

Four times we hear sounds rolling down quickly: 'This - is - my - mountain,' we all say together, while we bend our knees deeply four times and make the shape of the mountain with our hands.

The rumbles continue and we repeat our stamping while we bend forwards.

Then we hear eight drumbeats while firmly swinging our arms forward and backward, simultaneously or alternating left-right.

The swinging movements deepen, *hips and knees also join in*. You are allowed to loosen up your whole body. This might be a little awkward at first but it is very important for general suppleness. The mountain increases in size and width and your body experiences its own style. .

0.36

The eruption

The mountain becomes bigger and bigger and then suddenly there is an eruption. We stretch our arms and throw the lava and stones up in the air. Use all your energy and let everything go!

0.46
1.04

Repeat, a little faster.

1.09

Stones and lava

It is time to shake up your body again. Arms and shoulders shake and tremble simultaneously, from top to bottom and to and fro. We could also rotate on the spot. Shaking is good for a total relaxation and it also makes you giggle.

1.27

Thunder and lightning

We take a deep breath and spread our arms in the air and excitedly hold our breath for a second. Next we collapse in a flash without falling over. Do this as many times as you like while the rumbling continues slightly at the bottom of the mountain.

1.45

Rain

The thunder moves away slowly. In the distance we can hear the heavy shower coming, changing naturally into rhythmical drips. We bend our wrists up and down and we can simultaneously hop on the spot or round and round. In doing so we show that it is raining everywhere: nearby and far away... behind your back... over your head... While dancing you continue to bend and stretch your wrists as well as you can.

* The music of the Volcano can be compared to a dynamo. It starts off the movement and becomes stronger and stronger. In order to prepare the children carefully you could initially accompany the movements with a drum. Then the music begins very slowly.

Write Drawing

The mountain

When the mountain begins to rumble we move our hands and fingers, with or without chalks or crayons, at the bottom of the board or paper, making quick little squiggles up and down. Don't tap, we will do that later for stones and lava. Next we allow the hands to slide from top to bottom, while reciting with rolling sounds: 'This-is-my-mountain.'

When we hear the drumbeats we begin to wave arms in the same way as we did in the big space, but now we continue to touch the surface with our hands, chalks or crayons: from top to bottom to make the mountain bigger and fuller. Don't forget to bend your knees. The mountain rises 'from your toes'.

Children will usually begin drawing lines up and down. Ask them repeatedly to draw lines downward only.

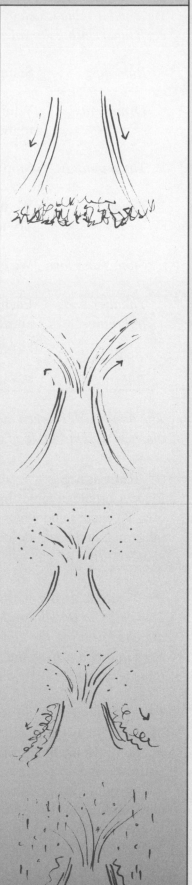

The eruption

Hands, chalks or crayons will slide from low down to high up across the surface after which arms continue to be stretched high up in the air. Say 'Go away, go away..!' We stretch our arms with enthusiasm from the hips, alternating left and right, or both simultaneously. The knees bend rhythmically. The eruption is thus represented by a collection of quick upward movements and lines.
Repeat.

Stones and lava

We make the stones and lava around the mountain come down while tapping with both hands. Thus they become small dots. Our feet are allowed to join in. The adult will count to sixteen out loud if the music is not always audible in a big group due to the loud tapping. That is how we can hear the thunderstorm arriving.

Thunder and lightning

We take a deep breath, hold it a moment and then let the lava and stones role down in wavy or looped lines. We blow fiercely over the paper to extinguish the fire or make sounds to go with it. Show how much strength and energy you have in your body.

Rain

We bend and stretch our wrists to the rhythm of the music and occasionally touch the surface. Now they become dashes instead of little dots. Dashes could also be made just above the paper every now and again (low doodling). That is how we focus more on our wrists. Simultaneously try to hop from one leg to the other.

❀ Volcano Dance, with music, CD 1

We stand in a big wide circle. The challenge is to look carefully at each other and to be tuned into each other during the Volcano Dance, as if producing choreography for a contemporary ballet

Rumbling	Stamp your feet without moving from your place and shake your arms.
Drumbeats	While waving our arms we walk eight counts in a line to the right or to the left.
The mountain	Stop and face the centre. Make the shape of the mountain four times.
Eruption	We turn round and make the circle wider while jumping and dancing. Try to make another good circle.
Stones and lava	We quickly make pairs and walk around each other while shaking.
Thunder and lightning	Each couple turn their backs to each other and with our arms and entire bodies we represent the thunder and lightning. Inhale deeply and breathe out forcefully.
Rain	We jump or hop following each other in a circle.

The dance will be even more attractive if we wear orange t-shirts and wave yellow, orange and red ribbons made of crepe paper.

❀ Rain dance

Place a couple of tables in a line or in a square close to each other. All the children make their own Volcanoes and when it begins to rain they leave their music drawing, dance around the table and let the rain descend around the other Volcanoes while finger dancing. If this proceeds satisfactorily, we can use chalks or crayons and make Volcanoes *together* in this way.

❀ Write drawing without music, but counting

Two children standing side by side take turns working on a big sheet of paper which has been attached firmly to the table. Both have two crayons in their hands but some extra crayons have been laid in a tray on the table or chair near to the working surface. Attach the tray firmly with a piece of Blu-Tack. We take turns and wear masks or tie scarves over our eyes.

Child A starts with the 'squiggle rumbles' of the mountain after which he puts the mountain down while waving his arms and counting out loud to eight. Then he takes a step to the side but he keeps his finger in the place where he has drawn the mountain.
Child B takes over the write drawing and repeats the previous movements and once again counts out loud to eight.
Now child A feels for the box of crayons and takes two new colours and draws the eruption in eight counts. Child B does exactly the same.
This is how we continue. Children A and B taking turns:

Stones and lava	Sixteen counts
Thunder and lightning	Four counts.
Rain	Sixteen counts. *Don't forget to hop... without falling!*

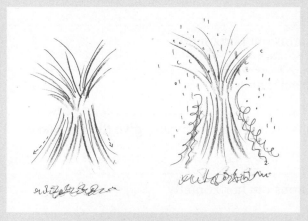

Foundation drawing

Story drawing

Text	Movements in the air
Holca volca, holca volca,	1. Wave your arms to and fro, bend your knees deeply
Holca Volca bellowed lava Lava all around	2. First waving movements, then arms stretched upward
It glowed and rolled right down	3. Arms roll downward
From scorching earth and burning tree	3. Arms and hands make bobbing movements
Tigers, rats and foxes flee Ashes, mud and red-hot clay	4. Hands make jumping movements
How I'd like to fly away!	5. Arms like wings

Rumbledeeboom, rumbledeeboom	1. Slap your thighs quickly
Lava, fire they split asunder Burning, churning, blunder. Thunder	2. Throw your arms out horizontally or stretched upward
Shhhhh...	3. Give your whole body a shake
The heavens start to open	4. Stretch up your arms
Keep on running – hoping	5. Running on the spot
Thunder, lightning, gloomy light Close down hatches, shut eyes tight (x2)	6. Hands as blinkers

The rainfall, the rainfall	1. Bend wrists and hop
Drive the sea of flames away	2. Throw arms out horizontally
Away, away, away	3. 'Throw out' hands
May the water downward tumble! Let the lava no more rumble!	4. The arms are falling downward, give them a shake
Be gone all fear and pain!	5. Throw arms out horizontally
Let us be in peace again!	6. Arms stretched upward

Write Drawing	Illustrations
1. Make a mountain with bobbing movements	
2. Lines down, lines up	
3. Waves down	
3. Waves down	
4. Short arches	
5. Horizontal lines to and fro at the top	

Write Drawing	Illustrations
1. Squiggle to and fro or stipple	
2. Eight lines up	
3. Squiggle to and fro	
4. Lines up	
5. Dashes to and fro or stipple	
6. Hands (still holding chalk) over the eyes	

Write Drawing	Illustrations
1. Short dashes everywhere and if possible hop simultaneously	
2. Draw lines away from you	
3. Hands over the ears	
4. Lines towards you	
5. Draw lines away from you	
6. Arms stretched upward and turn towards audience	

The rain has changed to thick fog and the Write Dance people walk along wriggly tracks over mountains and through valleys, past rocks, swamps and dense forests. They shuffle along feeling their way. The following morning after sheltering for the night in a deep cave the fog has lifted. They see a big open area in the distance in blazing sunshine. That is where they could build a new Write Dance village.

Full of courage they continue their journey. But suddenly they stop. In the distance they see something move. When they have come closer they see that they are animals. They are very special big animals with trunks, potbellies, lumps and very big toes. They waddle which is a funny sight and they are very friendly and tame. They allow themselves to be patted. Some children even climb onto their backs immediately. "These animals can help us carry stones and trees while building our new Write Dance village", says Kyalomo, the leader of the group.

Relaxation and rest, orientation, fantasy

- We feel our way and get our bearings in

    the big living area around us, the PE hall,
    the writing space around us behind our desks,
    the write drawing space on the (sensory-motor) surface.

- Our quest becomes an adventure.

- We will carry out this theme as slowly and relaxed as possible with our eyes closed. Racing and scratching are not good motor skills in this exercise. We learn to respect silence.

- The pieces of chalk or crayons are kept on the surface.

- Looped and bobbing movements without interruption are preparation for joining and connecting letters in handwriting.

- Movements need space. Shapes are discovered by using our imagination. We turn them into krongelidong-animals and give them names.

- Making krongelidong-animals is an interplay of lines giving confidence and helping you to write.

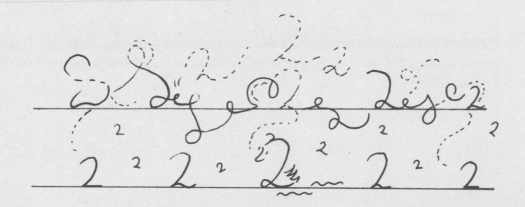

Number 2 *Random krongelidong squiggles on the surface emphasise curves and crossings. They are preparations for the curves and of number two.*

Movements in the air

Fog

We lie on the ground with our eyes closed, relaxed and listening to music.

Slowly but surely we get up and walk through the hall very slowly swerving and wriggling with our eyes open or closed. The arms join in as if we have to feel our way.

1.27
What's moving out there?

We slow down our steps because in the distance we can hear something rustle. What's moving out there? Making gestures we show that we are curious, but also a little frightened...

1.40
Krongelidong-animals

Now we will pretend we are the krongelidong-animals in the story. Arms hanging down loosely and swinging them slightly we walk round the hall. Here is someone else, moving differently. And another one..

2.20 And now we listen to the tune of the krongelidong song. We need to get used to it.

2.39 The music is repeated once more.

Variation One child thinks of movement, e.g. clumsy, waddling, crawling on hands and feet, shaking the head with big flapping ears to and fro, of with a dangling trunk...The others copy.

Write Drawing

Fog

First we listen to the music with our eyes closed. You could rest your head on your arms or let your arms float in the air. Next the fingers feel the surface, once again making wriggly movements, eyes remaining shut.

Then pause the music, the children take a piece of chalk or crayon in either hand, and the wriggling continues with eyes shut. To some children this still feels strange. Stand behind the child for a moment, place your hands on their wrists and help them a little.

Remind the children that the movements should be slow and looped, and be careful not to create too much pressure.

What's moving out there?

We open our eyes. We use facial expressions and gestures to express what we see in the distance

Krongelidong-animals

The first time we make this music drawing, we pause the music and prepare the krongelidong-animals step by step:

1. With our fingers we try to trace a line or find a track. A criss-cross of lines means that we may need to change direction. When there are fewer lines we can follow the track a little longer.

2. Trace one line with one piece of chalk or crayon and thicken it so that it becomes more visible. Repeat this twice or three times with other stretches of line.

3. While finger dancing connect the three stretches by following as many lines as possible. Continue to trace the same track with your fingers until you have mastered it.

4. Now follow the same track with one piece of chalk or crayon repeatedly, so that the lines continue to grow thicker and you see a shape emerging. This is the krongelidong-animal's torso.

5. Draw eyes, nose, ears, maybe whiskers, teeth, legs and tail. Your krongelidong-animal is born!
A krongelidong animal could also have two or three heads..., and several legs and tails...

Variation Another way of creating a shape is by looking for three or more crossings of lines. The crossings need to be thickened and then you should find a shape while finger dancing.

❀ Krongelidong-animals

1. The adult makes a soft rushing sound, for example by beating an object on a drum and she makes her voice sound mysterious. The children move slowly past each other and stop to one or several drumbeats, trying to keep their backs, necks, hips, arms, hands and wrists as still as a statue. The rushing continues and we will repeat this several times.

2. One child thinks of a silly 'krongel-walk' and another child copies and follows. This is how we set up krongelidong pairs or even a whole line of krongel animals.

❀ Eyes open, eyes shut

Think of all kinds of games to help the youngest children get used to closing their eyes.

❀ Owl face in pairs

This is a fun game which I remember well from my own childhood.

Adult and child, or two children will sit close together and just like Eskimos their noses touch. Slowly they recite together: 'eyes open:'…, their eyes are opened wide, 'eyes shut' … their eyes close, and then suddenly with a short cry we say: 'Owl face!' opening our eyes as quickly and wide as possible. It really feels as if you are looking into the owl's eyes of the other person! Take turns with other 'owls' and you will learn to look into each other's eyes!

❀ Leader and follower

In the area

Child A leads and child B puts their hands on child A's shoulders. To the music they slowly shuffle through the fog. We could also do so by closing our eyes or wearing an eye mask. Krongelidong-animals: Child B now continues its own way, inventing its own movements, copied by child A.

On board and paper

Children A and B sit facing each other at the table.

Child A is wearing the eye mask and child B is directing A's writing hand in a fantasy shape and consolidates the shape by tracing it several times. Child A is completely relaxed and allows B to take the lead.

When the shape is clearly visible, child A, still wearing an eye mask, is allowed to draw in the eyes, ears, nose, etc. Next children A and B (with their eyes open) complete the animal: colouring, consolidating, cutting out and sticking.

We will repeat it, but this time with the roles in reverse.

❀ Mother and child

We will divide the children into two or three pairs, all consisting of a krongelidong-mother and her krongelidong-child. The krongelidong-children are blindfolded. Together the pairs invent a soft sound. The 'animals' disperse in the room. Start the music for a moment indicating that it is time to start the game and then stop it. Now the mothers begin to call their children gently by the agreed sound. The child answers with the same call. Feeling their way and listening carefully to each other, the children try to find their mothers, wriggling their ways towards them.

❁ Birds and bicycles

Child A will draw five figures on the blackboard or on a big sheet of paper, e.g. a house, a tree, a car...

Child B puts on the eye mask and tries to move slowly with a piece of chalk, a crayon, a wet finger or a pencil and to draw a circle round the figures.

Child A will help him by giving directions: a little upward, downward, be careful, not too quickly, etc... When all the figures have circles round them they change places.

You can move forward in little birdlike patters or by cycling in loops, or moving awkwardly like a robot...

Also do this while finger dancing on a wet board or with a stick, peg or mini car in slippery paint. The prints will be wonderful!

Foundation drawing

Story drawing

Text	Movements in the air
We are the krongelbeasties Butterflies and centipedies We are a krongelidong… A ting, a tongue and a plingeliplung	1. Krongelidong wriggles 2. Arms stretched upward 3. Touch head and tongue, turn your wrists and end up in the air
Chorus Kringeli, krangeli krongelidong, Hairy, scary, nose and tongue (x2)	4. Walk around in a circle
We are the krongelbeasties Butterflies and centipedies We keep changing shape all the while We simply must have the latest style	1. Krongelidong wriggles with your whole body 2. Hands up in the air, face like a question mark
Kringeli, krangeli, krongelidong, Hairy, scary, nose and tongue (x2)	3. Walk around in a circle
Once an elephant said toot a toot too He kronckled here and then kronckled there And he made such a hullabaloo Then finally a trunk he grew	1. One arm like a trunk, supported by the other arm 2. Two arms stretched up into the air
And so he changed himself to a great big Snabant!	3. Arms stretched upward
Kringeli, krangeli, krongelidong, Hairy, scary, nose and tongue (x2)	4. Walk around in a circle
And there was once a giraffe and He kronckled here and then kronckled there And I sometimes had to break out in a big laugh When he showed to me his benden knee	1. Krongelidong wriggles 2. Singing 3. Bend knees
And he changed himself into a Pliaf!	4. Arms stretched upward
Kringeli, krangeli, krongelidong, Hairy, scary, nose and tongue (x2)	5. Walk around in a circle
And there was once a big huggy bear and he kronckled here and he kronckled there Then he suddenly didn't know what to wear but a hat made him an aristocrat	1. Give the impression of a bear: fat cheeks and strong arms Krongelidong wriggles with your entire body 2. Hat: flat hand on your head and up and down in the air
And so he changed himself into a Dandy Bear	3. Arms stretched up in the air
Kringeli, krangeli, krongelidong, Hairy, scary, nose and tongue (x2)	4. Walk around in a circle

Write Drawing	Illustrations
1. Draw krongelidongs on the board e.g. with a sponge 2. Arms stretched upward 3. Dot to the left, dot to the right and a circle with both pieces of chalk 4. Make circles with both hands	
1. Dance krongelidongs with your fingers 2. Turn round to the public arms stretched up in the air 3. Finger dancing or circling around with sponges	
1. Make an ear, head and trunk 2. Quickly draw a trunk 3. Hands holding pieces of chalk up in the air 4. Dry the write drawing again with cloths or chamois sponges	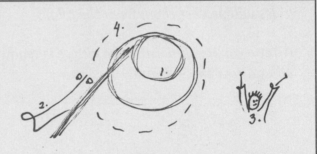
1. Krongelidong with fingers, chalk, sponges, cloths or chamois sponges 2. Wrists turned upward. 3. On a vertical surface: bend knees and stretch, don't move the chalk, lines appear by themselves! 5. Arms stretched upward 6. Quickly (with fingers, chalk, sponges, cloths or chamois sponges) make legs under the lines	
1. Make an upright eight and quickly draw circles attached to it like ears and four legs 2. Draw a hat! 3. Hands holding pieces of chalk up in the air 4. On the board: Clear everything with sponges making krongelidongs. On paper: circle round and round, around the drawings	

Kyalomo has chopped down a big tree in the woods and helped by the krongelidong-animals they put it in the centre of the big field. "This is a sundial which will help us tell the time and it will be the centre of our village," he says proudly. They tie a long rope to the pole and make Trunky, the biggest animal, walk round and round until it becomes a beautiful circle. This is followed by another four loops so that it became a beautiful eight-leaf clover.

The Write Dance people will grow vegetables and herbs in the southern loop because that is where there is the most sun. Beyond the eastern loop they will dig a huge lake because that is where the sun rises, which will make it very refreshing to have an early morning swim. In the West they build huts and houses which they cover in clay so that they can write draw on them, because the write dance people don't know any letters but draw everything they experience. In the North the animals can walk around freely. Their thick hides will protect them from the cold.

After a couple of months the village is ready and it has become more attractive than the village near the Volcano.

Round movements, crossings, melody

- Distinguishing between straight and round shapes is important. Letters are based on round and straight lines. Curves will take you round bends more easily than angles.

- Two circles side by side are the foundation of the horizontal eight, two circles above each other are the foundation of the vertical eight.

- Horizontal and vertical eights combined form an eight-leaf clover.

- In an eight-leaf clover we will find all the changes of direction which are repeated in letters and numbers.

- Managing contrasts such as over /under, left/right, encourages the bilateral coordination between the body and the halves of the brain.

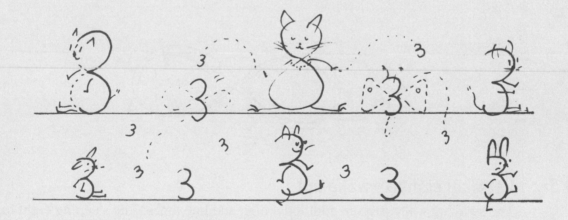

Number 3 *Number three is a semi-eight.*

Movements in the air

CD 3

Circles

Stand in a circle or spread out in the PE hall. Now use both arms to make big slow circles in front of your chest inward and outward. The shoulders join in and don't forget to bend your knees. Every now and then close your eyes.

Variation We can also make circles with our hips, head and wrists. Lying on the floor we turn our legs round in the air.

CD 4

Horizontal eights – sleeping

Place two hoops or other objects at a distance from each other in the room and make the group or a couple of children walk round them slowly in big eights. When the assistant gives us a signal we stop a moment and make big horizontal eights holding both hands together.
With both our hands under our cheeks we rock the horizontal eight asleep.

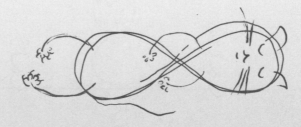

CD 5

Vertical eights – wake up!

The swaying waltz is given additional high and low tones. The sleeping eight has woken up. With both hands we draw vertical eights over our tummies and chests, and they become taller and deeper. Yawning is part of it too, as it is good for your supply of oxygen. In the end the eight will stretch from far above the head down to the floor. The vertical eight is awake and ready now!

CD 6

an Eight-leaf Clover

The music is becoming rounder because more instruments have joined in. We split the group in halves or walk along in pairs.
Add two hoops so that they make a square with the other hoops. One group of children walks along the horizontal eight and the other along the vertical eight. If all goes well there will be a beautiful sequence of walking, waiting, fitting in and adjustment.

Write drawing

Circles

1. Standing behind our desks we will make circles with both hands in the air. Don't forget to bend your knees.
2. Fold the paper into two halves.
3. Continue circling, one circle on each half. You could even sit down while doing this but do let your torso join in. Every now and again a foot may join in, or even your neck. If it feels good, close your eyes. Every now and again bring the crayons together, first in one circle, then in the other and occasionally lift your hands while you continue to draw circles. It would be good to alternate the crayons between left and right to mix the colours.

We also draw the circles as inward spirals and out again and in reverse.

Horizontal eights – sleeping

1. First feel along the diagonal lines with your fingers.

2. Draw a cross of about 10cm in the centre.

3. Join the circles in horizontal eights while finger dancing.

4. Draw horizontal eights with two crayons close to each other, close your eyes again every now and then and remember to raise your hands. First we allow the children to find their own way, but a little help in the right direction might be needed. Stand behind the child and place your hands on their wrists.

Eights in different shapes are quite common at first.

Without any music we call out the directions slowly, for example: 'to the door, to the window' or mention opposites such as 'sun and moon', 'summer and winter'.

Vertical Eights – wake up!

We turn over the paper and turn it a quarter, divide it into halves and draw one circle at the top and one at the bottom and connect them into vertical eights. We could also work on the board with sponges only and then with our fingers until the surface is dry.

The Eight-leaf Clover

An eight-leaf clover is created by joining-up a horizontal and a vertical eight. We start with a horizontal eight, add two circles and allow the movement to run smoothly from top to bottom and from left to right. Matching the movements we say out loud:
'Sleep, sleep..., night, night…, wake up, wake up, it is half past eight!'
When repeating this on large or small scale we could also draw a straight cross with four circles at each end. In that way you prevent the eight-leaf clover from being flat.

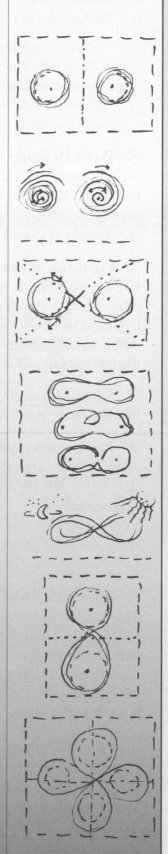

❀ **Rock-a-by Baby...**

Two children lie in one line with approximately five metres between each other. Other children walk round them in eights. They will sing one of the following five variations of 'Rock-a-by Baby' and when the song has finished the sleeping children wake up and make the movements matching the animals across the hall. Now two other children lie down on the floor and go to sleep

Rock-a-by kitty   *A cat with cat's eyes walks in big loops...*
Rock-a-by monkey   *A monkey with long arms, who warms me at night...*
Rock-a-by little goat   *A goat with long legs who jumps all over the place...*
Rock-a-by little cock   *A cock with beautiful feathers, who can teach you Write Dance...*
Rock-a-by little horse *A horse with long legs standing on my toes, ouch...*

❀ **Write Drawing and doodling**

We will make circles and horizontal, vertical and eight-leaf clovers. We start with both hands, one hand will be doodling in the air and will make the same movements as the write drawing hand. Then alternate hands.

Variation: the doodling hand makes movements across the face.

❀ **Eight-leaf clover: collaborating and adjusting**

Use the table board, slippery paint, shaving foam, sand or attach a big piece of paper to the table. Child A stands on the long side of the table, child B stands on the short side. Child A begins to make a vertical eight (possibly circles first); B also makes a vertical eight. Collaboration and adjustment will create a beautiful eight-leaf clover. Also try with sponges only on the table board and with your fingers until the board is dry.

❀ **Faces, glasses and owls**

We will draw small, tall, short, fat... bodies under the horizontal eights.

❀ **Feeling and experiencing**

A child 'write draws' round the eyes of another child with some cotton wool balls and says, 'left-right...left-right', then across the forehead and the nose or across the chin, 'over-under, over-under...'

Replace the cotton wool balls with face paint as a change!

Back: massage gently in circles, eights and eight-leaf clovers on each other's backs taking turns, which is a wonderful feeling!

❀ **Diagonals with three fingers**

This is a fine motor skill challenge where we work with one crayon.

Finger dancing: with only our thumbs, forefingers and middle fingers close together we make a couple of diagonals in both directions over each other. Next we only do this with our forefingers and then only with thumbs and middle fingers. After that we pick up the crayon between thumbs and middle fingers and make the diagonals visible in colour, to and fro, time and time again.

A little more difficult, very slowly: the forefinger begins at the top half of the diagonal and when the three fingers reach the centre of the area, the crayon, still held between thumb and middle finger, draws a line of approximately 10cm. Immediately after thumb and middle finger are raised approximately one cm above the surface and the forefinger continues its route alone. The forefinger is the 'pilot', while thumb and middle finger are the followers.

❀ Mask-girl / Mask-boy

We draw a simple girl or boy starting from a ball and a triangle. We can use two crayons on a big surface or just one pencil on A4-paper.

1. Volcano music. Rumbling mountain: rumbling underfoot.

2. We draw bold lines to the beats of the mountain to represent the dress or the trousers.

3. Explosion: Fire /suns / or hurray-rays.

4. Walk/krongelidong music: we draw krongelidong lines to represent the lace on the dress, embroidery and flowers, or stitching for the boy.

5. We draw the face in circular lines to a piece of Circle and Eights-music to create a mask or a pair of glasses.

6. We draw the arms, hands, legs and feet to a piece of Robot-music... finished! Then we add all kinds of drawings.

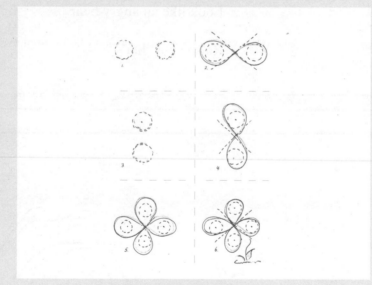

Foundation drawing

Story drawing

Text	Movements in the air
Just look what I've found A pretty pot so round And a wooden spoon just for stirring For stirring And a wooden spoon just for stirring In the pretty pot so round.	1. . Pretend you are stirring in a pot with a wooden spoon Or: hook each others arms two by two and turn around
And the pebbles are round And the sea-shells are round And I'm getting as hungry as a hound Eggs and flour and some honey sweet… stir the wooden spoon Let's have a treat!.	1. Turn your wrists 2. Pretend you are passing the wooden spoon to someone else with possibly a little courtesy
We'll feed up the bear, with some healthy food so sweet and very good… for you!! He'll stop his growling And even his scowling Although he might scare he's my Dandy Bear!	1. Draw circles over your tummy 2. Look like an angry bear 3. Raise your 'hat'

Write Drawing	Illustrations
1. Continue on the board: dry the previous in circles with a cloth until 'dry' 2. New theme: circling around with pieces of chalk	
1. Draw circles in a line just like stones or shells. 2. Then add a slanting line upward on top of each circle so that they become wooden spoons	
1. Quickly draw a bear from a vertical eight and four (or more) circles like in the previous song. 2. Lines towards you. 3. Draw a hat or turn to the audience and raise your 'hat'.	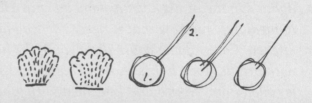

...

One morning Akito and his sister Inu wake up hearing strange noises. "Bang, bang, groan, groan, ding ding, tick tock..."

"It's as if I see big eyes, Akito, and hands and feet looking like little cupboards, come let's go and have a look" says Inu who isn't afraid of anything. Suddenly they find themselves standing in front of a robot, just as big as themselves and who has all kinds of flashing lights. On top of his head a small lid with 1L on it, is clanging up and down. Akito immediately realizes that it needs some oil and fetches some sunflower oil from the kitchen. Carefully he pours the oil onto the head and immediately the eyes begin to shine with bright green lights. A small hatch opens in his chest where they can see a film. "He is called Boro!" Akito and Inu shout with great enthusiasm, "And he is thanking us for rescuing him. A good pint of sunflower oil will help him on." They take him into the shed where he is free to do what he likes. When Akito and Inu arrive home that afternoon from their small village school they immediately go to the shed. They peep through a slit and they can see what is happening. Boro is busy making something with pumps, hoses, tins and trays, wheels and cogs. "What do you think he is making?" asks Inu. "Let's not bother him, it will sort itself out," says Akito.

Straight movements, beat and structure

- Straight lines and angles give a sense of stability and perseverance, and encourage concentration.

- We count out loud, with or without music. We feel strong. *I want to and I can do!*

- Straight lines and angles create firmness, but handwriting without curves points to inadequate fine motor skills and/or emotional blocks.

- In this Robot theme we experience healthy tension, we wake up and feel ready!

- We make straight lines or squares with two arms inward or outward. Don't forget your knees.

- We will practice with sensory-motor materials and on big sheets of paper. Don't forget to do some finger dancing first!

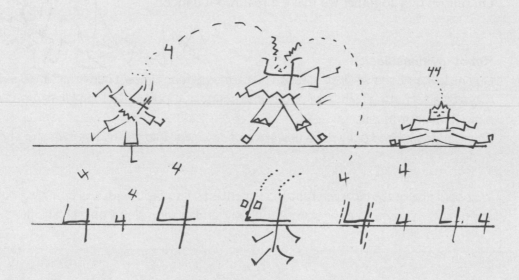

Number 4   *In the Robot we will draw straight lines and angles. We will recognise them in the number 4.*

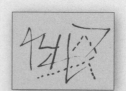

Movements in the air

0.00	**Boro the Robot** The music begins with four short, low notes repeated twice to which the robot sets himself in motion. We take slow, heavy and stiff steps and might count along.
0.30	Now the robot increases his step, and the assistant can count along. The children make accompanying sounds. Arms, elbows, shoulders, head and neck... all join in. Music is the source of inspiration!
0.51	**Lights and lids** The tones will now become higher and lighter and we may express this in smaller movements: short jerks with your hips, fingers and maybe stretch your toes and bend them. Shut your eyes tightly and open them again to the rhythm of the music.
1.13	**Robot dance** On our own or together we make a real robot dance!

Robot-gymnastics:
On the lower notes we first stretch our arms up four times, then four times sideways or alternating high-low / out-in and count out loud up to four. First practise this slowly, without music.
Four times we bend our wrists upward and downward to the high notes and then out and in.

We could alternate between fast movements to the fast beat and counting out loud (one - two - three - four) or counting 'slowly' and moving along: only to the first count.

Write Drawing

Boro the Robot

Big long lines: both hands together or alternating between height and width, anywhere in the middle or along the edges.

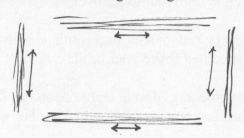

Lights and lids

We draw smaller (finger)dashes up and down, alternating with stipples randomly across the surface. After a little experience we will try small squares too. This could also be done with one piece of chalk or crayon. Allow yourself to be led by music in your personal expressions.

Robot dance

Dance away with your pieces of chalk or crayons but remember to move your whole body in accordance. Lay down the chalks or crayons and continue dancing with your fingers. Change the chalks or crayons between hands, so that the colours mix. After a little experience you could also use a variety of colours.

Dance with chalk and sponges, arms and shoulders, feet and legs, fingers and toes!

Variation We only draw big or small squares in a variety of sizes, beside each other or mingled.
After enough practise we can connect the squares and the battlements of a castle.

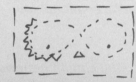

Tip:
Combine Circles and Eights with the Robot. First we will write draw horizontal and vertical eights which we then frame to the robot music.

Create variety with coloured pencils:
We create small angular movements, shark teeth or ragged mountain peaks around the horizontal, vertical eights or the eight-leaf clover. Every now and again switch back to the round music and to the figure of eight movements. It is a good listening exercise which also enhances eye-hand-ear coordination!

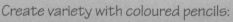

❋ **Robot-walk, without music but accompanied by counting and noises**
We will do this exercise slowly

1. Left foot first, right arm first and crooked; move forward slowly like a robot, the feet shuffle close to the floor. We will count to eight or to four twice over.

2. In four counts both arms move up in a jacked manner, and continue slowly up during four more counts until your arms are fully stretched above your head.

3. Allow your arms to drop sideways in little jerks during eight counts, until they are horizontal and then move them in a stretched and bouncy fashion like a robot with shock absorbers.

4. Slowly draw your arms sideways towards you in eight counts just like a bodybuilder. Show your 'robot cables'! Your arms then drop completely, the robot sinks in a heap, the battery is empty, the cables droop!

❋ **Old-fashioned clapping game, while counting**
We face each other in pairs and count out loud.

One-two-three-four.	Two pairs of hands clap each other
Five-six-seven-eight,	When you hear five and seven clap your own hands, at six and eight clap your partner's hands
Turn and turn and turn and wait	Both children rotate three times and when we hear '*wait*' we turn up our wrists, our elbows are crooked
We count out loud from nine to sixteen	In turns we clap our own hands and each other's left-right
You cannot be seen!	We open our eyes wide and then shut them tightly

❋ **A Crickle and a Cringle**

Child A makes a Crickle

Child B makes a Crickle in another colour, but in the same shape.

Child A makes a Cricklecrackle.

Child B makes a Cringlecrongle with another colour next to it.

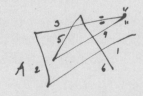

❀ Lines and squares

Fold a sheet of A3 paper into two halves down the centre. Then fold the left and right halves towards the fold. We now have three folding lines. We place three dots on each of the lines by using the helping hand to find the centre of each stretch of line. That is where the writing hand places a dot.
We draw three big squares in one line above the dots, several times on top of each other. It can also be done in sensomotor materials.

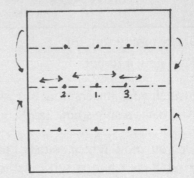

1. Let the squares 'run' or join them on the lower line (a) or as battlements (b)

2. Repeat the exercise by expanding the dots and with circles, running arches and swaying boats. You may also use the copy sheet (forerunner of the writing sheet)

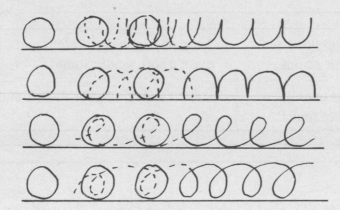

Foundation drawing

Story drawing

Text	Movements in the air
Teeny weeny tiny tot *I am now a ro-bot*	1. Robot-like movements
Stretch your fingers now out wide *And make a silly sound (x2)*	2. Stretch and bend your fingers and make a silly sound
Do you know which sounds I made? *Stretch your fingers with me now!*	3. Turn around and invite the audience to join in

Text	Movements in the air
Teeny weeny tiny tot *I am now a ro-bot*	1. Robot-like movements
Stretch your fingers out wide now *And make a silly sound*	2. Stretch and bend your fingers and make a silly sound

Text	Movements in the air
Teeny weeny tiny tot *I am now a ro-bot*	1. Robot-like movements
Stretch now both your arms out wide *And make a silly sound!*	2. Stretch and bend your arms and make a silly sound

Text	Movements in the air
Stretch now both your legs out wide *And make a soft and gentle sound*	1. Jump and spread your legs and make a soft, gentle sound
Stretch again your fingers out *And make once more a silly sound!*	1. Stretch and bend your fingers and make a silly sound

Write Drawing	Illustrations
1. Draw big lines up-and-down on either side of the surface	
2. Slanting lines and silly sound	
1. Turn around and invite the audience to join in	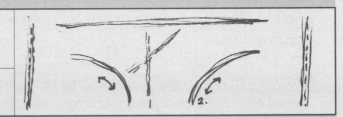
1. Draw big lines up-and-down on either side of the surface	
2. Slanting lines and silly sound	
1. Draw big lines up-and-down on either side of the surface	
2. Big horizontal lines at the top	
1. Make wide jumps, arms and hands join in and the pieces of chalk leave dots	
2. Slanting lines and silly sound	

Boro the robot is still working in the shed. After two days he has finished and leaves the shed taking big robot steps. Akito and Inu can't believe their eyes. They can see an enormous machine which looks like a very special locomotive. It has eight wheels and the steam coming from the front disappears through a hole in the roof upward. On top of the machine Boro has made two seats with coloured flashing lights around them. With his big steel arms he indicates that they should sit down. Akito immediately grabs the control stick and proudly drives out of the shed where an enormous crowd of Write Dance people has gathered to admire the machine. Akito drives it over a bumpy road without any tracks of course. Boro's eyes are now bright orange with excitement and he can even make little skipping jumps.

"We need to build a track," says Kyalomo. "There is lots of iron in the mountains. We need a good blacksmith and plenty of strong men in the village who can help. And in a few months the train will be able to travel miles".

Looped arcades and garlands, from slow to fast

- Loops emerge from rotating movements and crossing lines.
  They roll off the Train by themselves!

- Circling around to the left, movement to the right:
  loops upward.

- Circling around to
  the right:
  movements to
  the right:
  loops downward.

- Up and down are opposites we learnt doing the vertical eights.

- We extend the loop upward and downward.

- The garland is the symbol of openness,
  sharing, offering, communication, intuition.

- The arcade is the symbol of closeness,
  keeping to yourself, concentration.

- The letters are enclosed in the combination of garlands and arcades.

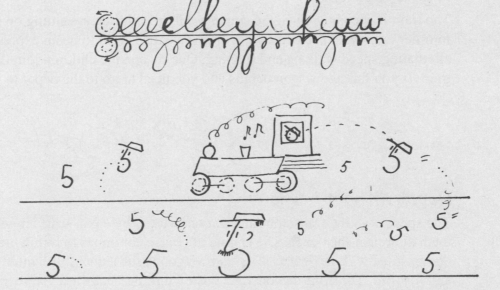

Number 5 *Number 5 often presents problems. If we can turn
it into a locomotive we will be able to remember
round and straight.
The train driver needs to eat well to be nice and
strong. Digging coal is hard work!*

Movements in the air

Station

We are standing behind each other in a line. When we hear the first station noises, we slowly set off.

1. Like an old-fashioned locomotive with crooked arms tight against the body, turning round from the shoulders.

2. Like a modern train by keeping the arms down in a relaxed manner and rotating the wrists. These are the wheels of the modern train. You could also alternate this by keeping the fists together and turning round, away from your chest.

0.12

Train

The train travels down the hall in any direction or along the sides. Objects or the bench by the wall can serve as stations. This is where we stop for a moment but the arms continue to turn very slowly, because after all the motor has not switched off.

0.47

Another station

A couple of passengers get on and off quickly. We could also pretend that the train has already left and that one or two passengers have arrived late! They will have to sit on the bench and wait until the next train arrives.

1.00

High Speed Train

The train is speeding down the country. All the children are sitting on seats. In order to prevent accidents we will first ask one child to be an express train, alternating speed walking and running. One by one the children join the express train. If you fall, the wagon derails and you need to go to the depot to be repaired.

Depot without music

The speed walking train stops at a station marked by e.g. a scarf anywhere in the hall or near the bench. The engine of course continues to turn which we can demonstrate with our wrists. The train wagon is subsequently shunted backward and forward. The arms demonstrate this by turning backward and then forward. Now we turn on the music and the train can go!

Write Drawing

Station

Both chalks or crayons, far apart or close to each other, circle around. You could also do this in the four corners. Without music we could stop the train there and we will invent the name of our destination.

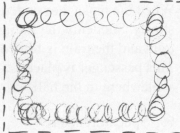

Train

The train leaves slowly, the loops are drawn in a line but are allowed to link each other. At other times we can draw loops side by side without them touching each other with or without music. It will create a little more tension but it is a logical succession and good for fine motor skills. The loops upward are beginning to look like joined-up letters e! We will follow the tempo of the music.

Another station

When we arrive at a station, we continue to rotate the chalks or crayons, even 'doodling low down', by raising the hand a little above the surface. All passengers must descend, and now we doodle high up in the air!

High Speed Train

We pick up another piece of chalk or crayon and the loops now race across the paper at high speed. At first it will be chaos but with a little exercise they can still remain on track. We could make that track for example with the music of the Walk, wriggling slowly through the whole country.
The High Speed Train will also stop at a station, just pause the music for a moment. First we stipple quickly away from the station, the people are getting off. Next we stipple quickly towards the station, where people are boarding the train. Then the train speeds on again.

Depot without music

Slowly we make loops forward and backward, but also up and down. Make accompanying sounds.

Variation *Raise or lower the volume of the music now and then for bigger and smaller loops.*

Derailment *The loops run off the board or off the paper, the arms drop down loosely, the body collapses…*

Without Music *A very old train. With a lot of groaning and squeaking it sets in motion.*

❀ **Indian raid**

Two groups: Train children and Indians

A long train of children or a group of three or four together initially chug up the mountain very slowly, panting audibly. Their arms turn round like the connecting rods of a locomotive. Next we switch on the music of the train song and the train rolls along through the hall. When the music has ended the train continues to chug further up another mountain, very slowly. Suddenly the Indian music (CD 27) is switched on. The Indians dance around the train and the train is forced to stop. One Indian has a skipping rope and chooses a passenger. This passenger is placed on the Indian's horse and is taken in a gallop to the Indian camp somewhere in the hall.

❀ **Special tracks**

With one coloured pencil we draw train loops round

1. horizontal, vertical eights or eight-leaf clovers,

2. squares,

3. big letters,

4. lines with wide spaces, such as an A3 page folded into four areas: horizontally from left to right or vertically from top to bottom.

Also try doing it with a wet finger on a very damp board until the board has dried or with the tip of a stick or a peg in slippery paint. The prints will be masterpieces!

❀ **Crying one minute, laughing the next**

Fold a large sheet in halves and attach it to the table.

Friends: we draw mirrored loops inward from top to bottom simultaneously with both hands and we draw friendly and laughing faces inside the loops.

Angry: we draw outward loops in another colour and turn them into angry faces.

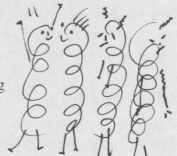

❀ **A train with 25–30 wagons**

We unroll an entire roll of wallpaper in the corridor. We choose a train driver who may draw the locomotive and the rest of the group draw passenger trains. We could also do this in the schoolyard. Play the music!

❀ **Travel game**

This will work similarly to the 'Birds and bicycles game' in the theme Walk / Krongelidong. Child A will draw five or more figures on the board of paper, e.g. a station, a house, a school… Child B puts on the eye mask and child A carefully turns child B round several times so that child B has lost some sense of direction. Then child A leads him carefully to the board or the sheet of paper and places child B's finger carefully on one of the figures. Child B travels accompanied by sounds from one figure to the next and is directed by child A who says 'to the left, to the right'.

By plane	a long line
By train	loops
Like a Robot	making awkward and angular movements
Like a boy or girl	in free movements, humming or singing

Variation: *Instead of spreading several figures across the paper, child A puts the figures at the beginning and end of three folded lines traced in pencil. Will child B succeed in following the line? Then we swap roles.*

❀ Puffing flower

On paper you can make a little flower out of 'train loops' while you breathe in and out slowly and audibly. The chalk, crayon or pencil movements match the breathing.

Don't do this too long because deep inhalations and exhalations could cause a child to feel dizzy.

❀ One puff forward, one huff backward

Say out loud: *puff-puff-puff*...if you make loops forward.
Say out loud: *huff-huff-huff*...if you make loops backward.
Raise a finger of your other hand for each loop, from your thumb to your little finger.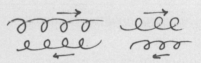

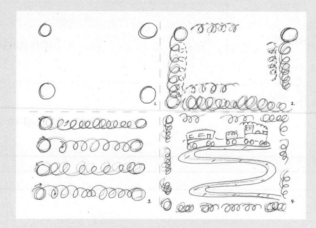

Foundation drawing

Story drawing

Text	Movements in the air
Choo-choo, choo-choo, choo-choo Choo-choo, puff, puff, puff We're chugging, lugging, chugging, Quite enough, nuff, nuff.	1. Follow each other and make locomotive movements
Psshhhh, psshhhh Take a rest now – here we stay	2. Stop here
Let the steam just gently fade away	3. Arms go up in the air

Text	Movements in the air
We're chugging, lugging, chugging Up and down Past mou-ountains and whee-eels Spinning 'round	1. Locomotive-movements
Psshhhh, psshhhh Take a rest now – here we stay	2. Stop here
Let the steam just gently fade away (x4)	3. Arms go up in the air

Write Drawing	Illustrations
1. On the board: with sponges or dry cloths draw loops upward or downward. On paper: draw loops along the edges 2. Turn wrists up 3. Bobbing lines upward	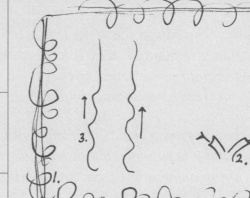
1. Draw reversed loops along the previous ones 2. Turn wrists up 3. Bobbing lines upward	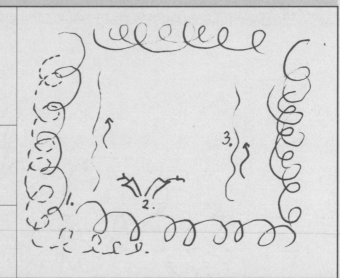

In the south of the village the Write Dance people have not only sown seeds of vegetable and herbs, but also planted trees. It has become an orchard of about one thousand trees. They aren't ordinary fruit trees, no they are a very special kind. They are the so-called seasonal fruit trees because you can pick fruit of these trees at any time of year.

In spring the trees are a beautiful orange with many oranges. When they have been picked bare and it is summer, bunches of juicy dark red cherries appear on the same trees. Then it is autumn and apple time. And in winter nuts grow on these trees.

Boro has designed a picking machine: a moving ladder with automatic grabbers. In winter the picking machine is repaired and cleaned and it is parked in the shed. The ripe nuts fall off the tree and are ready to be picked off the ground.

Movements upward and downward, loops all around

- Similar to the Volcano straight and circular lines alternate quickly.

- The young tree grows upward with some light pressure, but the trunk is drawn with strong pressure.

- The four branches give a sense of freedom similar to the Volcano's eruption. We pick the fruit at a high level and place all of them low down in the basket.

- The tree is the symbol of self-awareness, growth and development. The tree grows. Your body and experiences join in!

- The progress of your writing motor skills is closely related to the development of brain functions and personality.

- If the brains feel what you are doing, the rest will follow!

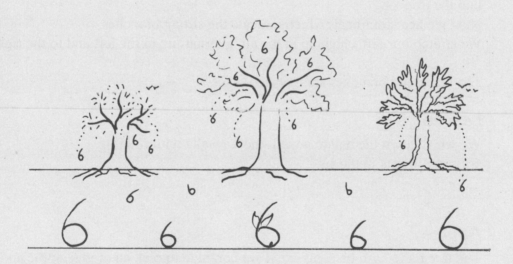

Number 6 Apples and their stalks or leaves drop off.

Movements in the air

0.16	### The maturing of the young tree We squat or bend over deeply. When we hear the first tones we hear how a small young plant grows into a young tree. We demonstrate this by slowly lifting our body and then spreading our arms wide.
0.30	### Twigs and leaves We show the thin twigs and leaves by making small waving gestures with a flexible wrist.
0.38 0.46	We repeat the growing plant and when the tones come rolling down, the arms descend too with slightly shaking wrists.
0.51	### The trunk and the branches We demonstrate with two downward arm movements that the tree has become tall and fat. Instead of a Volcano mountain it will now be a straight trunk. We can hug the tree too.
0.55 0.56 0.57 0.58	Next we hear four beats which indicate the strong branches. We stretch our arms high up in the air, alternatiing to the left and to the right. The trunk and branches are repeated twice.
1.10 1.42	### Leaves We whirl down the hall to a well-known waltz with rotating arms and wrists in the air.
1.25	### Apples The tree ballet will be complete if we continue to pick an orange/apple and placing this in a basket on the floor. We stretch and say 'high', grab the fruit and place it in the basket while we say 'low'.
1.58	### Cherries The grabbing movements now accelerate and we continue to pop cherries in our mouths

Write Drawing

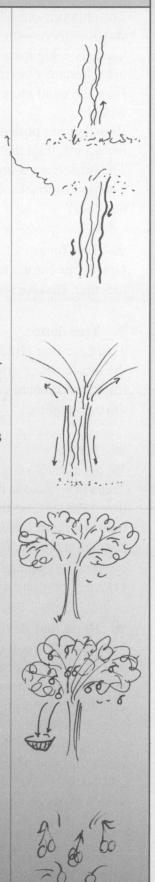

The maturing of the young tree

Two crayons or two pieces of chalk at the bottom of the paper or board. We draw some squiggles which represent seeds. Choose a seed that may grow into your tree. To the music you draw two very thin lines upward close together and very slowly. We do this twice.

Twigs and leaves

Small thin squiggles or to-and-fro dashes at the top of the young plant. Also draw leaves slowly while doodling high up in the big writing space around you.

Doodling just above the surface we lower the chalks or crayons. This is how we show that a couple of leaves are dropping.

The trunk and the branches

We use a little more pressure to draw two lines downward. That is the trunk. Shortly after we will draw four strong lines up for the branches. Start on the trunk halfway up the page because the branches still need to grow above them. We will repeat trunk and branches twice.

When the music drawing is complete, you might be able to draw some rings round the trunk, they are growth rings or an expression of your hugs.

Leaves

Loops everywhere around the branches represent the foliage. In contrast to the train it is now fine to mix them.

Apples

We quickly draw a small basket on the ground. We draw a few circles in the tree in orange or red and then 'lay' them in the basket.

Cherries

According to the story it is possible to have several fruits growing from the tree. We will draw two circles together in another colour. Later on you can add the stalks in pencil.

Repeat the music drawing while finger dancing and humming or singing simple words or parts of the song.

❀ Blow and wriggle exercise

The children stand in pairs. Child A is the tree and has bare feet. B is the wind. The tree is standing there with high arm-branches stretched wide and the wind-child blows through his hands holding them like a horn to his mouth while blowing gently round the tree... The tree's branches are swaying too, a few leaves dropping too...

Now the wind increases, there is going to be a gale! The tree is beginning to wobble and wobble...

Branches are pulled to all sides... and... first one foot-root comes up, then an arm-branch breaks off, then the next, and finally the tree gives in, falls down and lies there rigidly. The branch-arms are intertwined and stretched up past the ears.

The wind subsides and blows slowly against the bare root feet. Can the trunk lie rigidly on the floor?

❀ Tree forest

Unroll one or two rolls of wallpaper on the floor and create a very big Write Dance forest together. Can we see wood for trees? How many trees are there?

❀ Tree dance

There are four children, each standing behind a tree in a line or in a square. We switch on the music. After drawing the young tree each child moves up a seat. We repeat this after the trunk, the branches and the leaves. Then you will have returned to your own tree and you draw its apples.

❀ Jungle

We need trees, snakes, insects, monkeys and spectators.

Trees in a line, far from each other, snakes sliding down, insects finger dancing gently down the legs, up the back and back again tickling all the way up and down; monkeys jump between them starting from a squat with arms stretched wide. The wild monkeys jump right through the trees, four jumps forward and four jumps back... The spectators judge which monkey jumps the highest but also bends the deepest without falling over! The best monkey may rest now and allow itself to be defleaed. Now play the Rain Forest music (CD 28).

❀ Rigid and flexible trees

Put your eye mask on you head, but not over your eyes yet. Draw a long line of trees slowly and precisely, for example ten poplars at equal distances. This you should measure with three or four fingers using your other hand. Take another colour, place the finger of your assisting hand on the first tree and pull your eye mask over your eyes.

Now trace flexible trees over your rigid trees. Without looking you should measure the distance between the trees again using the fingers of your assisting hand. Take off the eye mask; did you place the flexible trees too close or too far from each other? Are the branches and leaves too high or too low? Complete your tree line with lots of colour and fantasy and then add birds, toadstools, pixies with your eyes shut.

❀ **Tiggy-twiggy and cherry-berry trees**

We will repeat the tree line once again in a similar fashion but now we sit facing each other. Discuss how many fingers you will place between each tree. One child's trees will fall in the space between those of the other child. This can also be done on a long stretch of wallpaper or wrapping paper.

We now invent fantasy names and draw them accordingly. For instance: a short willow grows into a tiggy-twiggy tree, a big pine tree, a cherry-berry tree (a Christmas tree, not with baubles but with cherries!) an oak tree, an okay-look out tree (a tree in which you can build a high tree house), etc.

Change places and both wear the eye mask. Child A will draw trees over child B's trees, trying to keep the same distance. Child B does the same over child A's trees. You could also discuss which tree you are going to draw, maybe you would like to add a rosy-posy tree...?

Foundation drawing

Story drawing

Text	Movements in the air
I'm a tree, look at me! Here I sta-and for you and for me I'm a tree, look at me! Here I sta-and for you and for me	Hug the tree and put down the trunk with both arms
Chorus Our... Branches branches... Swaying swaying... Leaves leaves... Waving waving... Wa-ving	Dance in circles with stretched arms and rotating wrists
Hurrah! I am strong and I see how I grow!	1. Elbows at an angle, show your muscles! 2. Stretch your arms
Chorus Our... Branches branches... Swaying swaying... Leaves leaves... Waving waving... Wa-ving	Dance in circles with stretched arms and rotating wrists
A pear and a peach! One for me and o-ne for each	Picking movements
Pick them high, lay them down And quickly put them in your mouth	Put them in your mouth

Write Drawing	Illustrations
Draw the trunk with both hands, chalk, sponges or chamois sponges	
1. Branches, left, right or both hands together 2. Looped leaves with both hands	
1. Elbows at an angle, show your muscles 2. Stretch your arms	
1. Branches 2. Looped leaves	
Small circles	
Bring your hands to your mouth (don't eat the chalk!)	

Write Dance people love adventure and are always exploring. This time a group of young people in sturdy hiking boots, carrying rucksacks, set out. Once again over mountains and through valleys, past rocks and through forests, but they are used to it now. At night they build a fire and snuggle up to each other under their blankets.

Very early one morning they are woken up by the sound of a bird. It's as if its big silver wings are two meters wide.

"It is an albatross", shouts Takoro, a young man who is always full of ideas. "The sea can't be far away now. The albatross will show us the right direction."

Full of courage the young Write Dance people continue their way singing and dancing until they finally reach the high sand dunes. Each time they think they see the sea, there is another dune… and another one… and another one. Their feet sink down in the warm sand but they are not discouraged!

And then Takoro is the first to see the sea. He sees the bright blue clear water and a broad pearl-white beach in front of him. He runs and summersaults down the dune as fast as he can and he dives into the refreshing water with a splash. "We are going to build boats," he says enthusiastically. "The robots and the krongelidong-animals will help us and we will build a train track right down to the beach. Tomorrow we will return to the Write Dance village to tell them the big news!"

Wavy movements, from lapping to stormy

• The sea music touches our senses: rest, excitement and safety.
  We experience space and freedom in the big seabird.

• We will divide a circle into two halves by means of a horizontal line.

  At the top you see a rounded shape: the letters m and n.

  At the bottom there is a hollow shape: uvw   the letters u, v and w.

• If we alternate the hollow and the rounded shapes beside each other it will
  create a wavy movement. Not all children can immediately cope with these
  contrasts. They usually choose the simpler arched movement.
  We can solve this by placing circles in a line as a support.

• We can make waves horizontally, as well as vertically, which will be the
  foundation of the letter s.

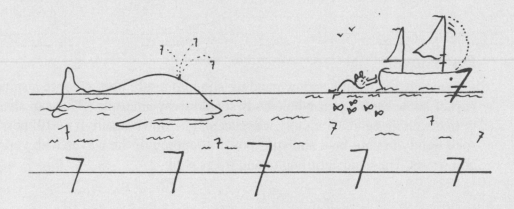

Number 7 *We cut through the waves with the bow of our ship.*

Movements in the air

The sea level

We lie quietly on the ground and hear the calm sea music. This can be demonstrated by arms floating slowly from side to side. The sea is as smooth as a mirror.

0.46

A bit of wind

Slowly the wind rises and very carefully we get up and sit on our knees. The arms now sway increasingly and the torso rocks along too.

1.08

More wind

The wind increases, we get up and begin to walk slowly between the objects and our arms now make gentle bobbing movements. Bobbing movements to and fro can change into horizontal eights.

1.12

Gale!

It's gale force! We demonstrate this by making diving movements with both hands like a ship dipping down into the waves. Of course we let the wind blow fiercely through the room.

1.37

Safe haven

Fortunately the wind lies down and we slip into a safe port. Choose a suitable corner in the room. Your whole body should sway smoothly. This can also be done with a wobbly head. Gradually we relax and lie down again. It is still possible to rock lightly in your boat and you show the lapping of the waves with your hands and wrists. The head is rolling to and fro as well.

1.48

Little Tea Ship…

The music changes into the first beats of the song 'Little tea ship'. In *More Write Dance* this music will be enhanced and we will make a separate music drawing of the 'Little Tea Ship'. It is very appropriate to do this after the sea theme.

Variation   *We will replace the waves with the wings of a big seabird, such as a seagull or an albatross. The bird is resting on the beach. We sit there relaxed, fully bent over and with our heads close to our knees, with our arms stretched backward. We make ourselves as small as possible. Then the bird rises very slowly, spreads his wings and flies across the sea and the wide ocean. After its adventure it returns to the safe beach and falls asleep with its head tucked away.*

Write Drawing

The sea level

At the bottom of the paper or on the table board we make a few lines from side to side. This could also be the bottom of the sea on which we could eventually use our fantasy with a coloured pencil.

A bit of wind

The waves begin to lap and the water begins to move. We will draw several stones in a line with the water lapping against them. Without any music we say 'above-under-above-under' or 'bobbeli-bobbeli...'

More wind

Now we stand up and first make bobbing movements with our arms and wrists in the air, and then draw waves on the surface. Don't forget to doodle waves low and high to encourage a complete release of tension. Draw another couple of stones or shells in addition.

Gale!

Let your body go, turn around, you could walk round your desk or quickly through the classroom, but then go back to your place to let the pieces of chalk or crayons dance over the high waves. If you have already completed the Cat theme the ocean waves will come in very useful now!

Safe haven

Choose a spot on your writing surface which is what your waves or your boat are heading for. Add the details later.

Little Tea Ship...

We sway from side to side in rocking motions on the same spot or we let the boat enter the harbour very slowly.

Fish dive *We draw a big seabird and a whole school of fish. Add the numbers. Close your eyes. Doodling high the big bird makes a couple of circles over the sea and then shoots down to catch a fish. What is the score! Try this in pairs too.*

❋ **Flatfish, rays and dolphins... with music**

Two groups: sea-children and fish-children. We use a strip of light material for the sea, pre-ferably in blue, turquoise or purple voile..., or all three!

Some children are lying quietly 'in the sand'. The voile is spread over them, the ends are held by some sea-children. The sea-children sit on their knees. When the music begins they make the soft swishing noise of the sea and stand up slowly as they let the sea sway over the bodies of the fish.

The flatfish begin to make light zigzag movements. The wind rises, the sea-children let the sea waft carefully and gently and the flatfish now change into big rays. They spread their 'floppy arms' very wide and move across the floor. A good shoulder exercise! More wind; the rays now change into dolphins, capering playfully and horsing and 'jumping' around the room. When the gale rises the sea-children leave their cloth and make big waves with their arms or whirl round the room like little tornadoes. The wind subsides and the fish and the water move to a safe haven where they can continue to bob along.

❋ **Sea surge**

Some children hold a big transparent tarpaulin with a little puddle of water in it. Put a piece of blue and green crepe paper in it. We move the tarpaulin very carefully to the music and the water becomes increasingly blue. When you lie under it you can see the water play yourself.

❋ **Paper boats**

Lie flat on your back. You are the sea and you make very small waves. Place a paper boat on your tummy and inhale deeply and audibly and then exhale. Your boat goes up and down.

❋ **Fish and fish...**

This is a good preparation for drawing loops in all directions.

Children A and B take turns and draw short and long dashes randomly across the surface, however, without touching each other.
Children A and B take turns to draw a loop on the dash, and it doesn't matter in which direction. After a bit of practice they should be able to draw a tail and a body in one line. Straight and round shapes alternate. Then children A and B finish the fish with lots of fantasy. In liquid watercolours or simply a blue coloured pencil (very light pressure!) it will turn into the deep sea or an aquarium. Don't forget plants, etc.

✿ **Deep sea diving**

Child A draws a treasure box with three pearls in it on sheets of A3 and A4 paper, including three silver coins and three bars of gold. The pearls consist of circles with dashes like rays around them, the coins are coloured circles and the bars of gold are squares. Size depends on the (table) board or paper. Child A closes its eyes and tries to find the valuable treasures with a finger, chalk, crayon or pencil. Child B keeps the score:

Pearl = 1 point   *Coin* = 2 points   *Bar of gold* = 3 points
Agree how many times you are allowed to 'pick'.

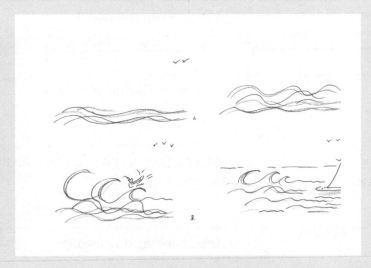

Foundation drawing

Story drawing

Text	Movements in the air
Take me along Oh mighty sea In my boat and far away (2x)	1. Arms bob from side to side
I guard all night	2. Tap your cap
Sleep now so tight	3. Rock your hand under your chin and head

Text	Movements in the air
The waves of the ocean Flow head over heel	1. Arms bob up and down
I've got the motion The motion I feel	2. Spin round flaying your arms
And I look and I looked And I saw and it seemed	3. 'Make a pair of 'binoculars' with thumb and forefinger
In the far off Of the deep of-the-peep That something had moved	4. Arms bobbing downward

| But that was you! | Point at each other |

Write Drawing	Illustrations
1. Make waves with fingers or pieces of chalk, sponges, chamois sponges, cloths...	
2. Tap your cap	
3. Smaller waves or horizontal eights	

Write Drawing	Illustrations
1. Big waves and move your whole body	
2. Big waves	
3. Two small circles together	
4. Waves downward	

Write Drawing	Illustrations
Turn round, look at each other or at the audience	

Balimo the woodcutter, Calima, the tailor, Salina the artist and Xaleron the carpenter have remained on the beach while the others have walked back to the Write Dance village. Calima and Salina use shells, stones and sticks to draw pretty rings in the warm sand. Xaleron has found a couple of big pieces of wreckage of a fishing boat and is trying to calculate the size of the boat.

A week later a big group of Write Dance people returns with Takoro and Trunky in front. Everybody has brought tools to build a strong boat and Calima will make the sail.

After some weeks the boat is finished and eight men are chosen to try the boat. But as soon as they are out at sea a strong gale rises and the boat is threatening to sink. "We won't manage!" says frightened Xaleron. "We will drown!" But no sooner does he say this when the almost shipwrecked boat appears to be lifted up from the water. "What is this? Look we are pushed along by big water cats, they look like lions!" Balimo calls to the others. "They have come to save us!" There are also small water kittens plugging the holes in the boat with their paws. And that is how the men arrive back on the beach safely, and fall asleep exhausted, warm and safe against the big water cats.

Three quarter circles, to and fro and joined

- Joined three quarter circles encourage suppleness and resilience. Compare this to developing your style in sports such as tennis and golf.

- The three quarter movement is important in preparation of the letters a, c, d, g and q.

- We can see cats' heads but also ocean waves in the three quarter circle movement.

- First we focus on some three quarter circles which we can turn into cats' heads.

- Once we have mastered the movement, we can make a whole line of ocean waves.

- Ocean waves can also be created by 'pushing' half a circle forward and gradually extending it into a three quarter circle.

Number 8 *We turn number 8 into cats. We could also link up the heads of the eights in a long line.*

Movements in the air

Circles

The music begins with the circle music as we have heard in the music theme 'Circles and Eights'. But now the melody continues differently. It is a good listening exercise to distinguish both circle melodies.

0.48

Arched swings

The saxophone is now playing an inviting swinging rhythm to which we make big arches over our heads. As a variation we could also continue to make the arches smaller, drop the arms like windscreen wipers in front of our faces and then doing the same with our wrists and our forefingers in front of our noses. Our whole body needs to continue swinging in these smallest of movements and don't forget to miaow!

± 1.18

Cats' heads

We stroke our heads with two paws. They are given a good wash too. We start at the neck and slide over the head down to the nose which we pinch gently and then say 'miaow'. We will do this to the beat of the music and don't forget to bend your knees rhythmically.

Some children soon find out that you can take a short-cut by allowing one hand to slip past the ear. That is not a problem but on the surface they need to be three quarter circles.

Now and then place your hands on your hips and bend from left to right or from front to back.

1.24

Cat-swings

The pace increases and takes us into a good jazz-swing. However we do continue to concentrate on the to-and-fro movement.

If we have already practised the ocean waves on paper or with sensory-motor materials, we could also practise them with our arms in the air.

Write Drawing

Circles

We will stand behind our desks but halfway through your music drawing you may sit down too.
Similar to the theme Circles and Eights we fold a big sheet of paper down the centre lengthwise, draw two dots and circles round them.

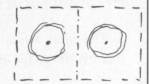

Arched swings

Hold one or two chalks or crayons close together and separate the circles by a horizontal line. We will draw arches over the upper halves of the circles. Try first in the big writing space over your head and gradually move down to the surface. You could also draw the arches outward and back in again..

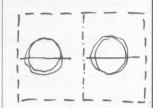

Cats' heads

We will place a clearly visible dot on the right where the circle cuts across the line. It is the cat's nose.

Hold one or two chalks or crayons close together and separate the circles by a vertical line. Place another dot on the lower crossing of lines. It's the beginning of the cat's neck. We will also draw eyes, ears and whiskers.

Holding one or two chalks or crayons close together you now make a three quarter circle, from the neck to the nose. The nose is very important, each time we have arrived there we say 'miaow' out loud! That is how it remains a true three quarter circle.

Cat-swings / Ocean-swings

Place a slanting line between the two cats' heads and join them swinging, to and fro and back again, first with one piece of chalk, or one crayon, then two. After a little practice you could draw a couple of cats' heads in a line. Don't forget to miaow. And of course we could create the heads of other animals and make them bark, grunt and cock-a-doodle-do.
We could also call this similar movement Ocean wave. We should first run the three quarter movements smoothly to the right, similar to the arched swings. We then pull the waves apart so that they no longer cross each other. If we don't prepare the ocean waves with round cats' heads, they will flatten and sharpen into the fins of a shark or the spines of a hedgehog. This exercise is important to enhance general suppleness and in preparation of the letters a, c, d and g.

Variation *Nod your head at each arch of your cats' heads or ocean waves.*

❀ **Cat-yoga**

We will do these exercises on a soft surface. The more slowly we do this exercise the better the cat will feel its muscles.

1. The cat is asleep rolled up in a ball, then wakes up after a moment and stretches its paws one by one as far as possible.

2. Now the cat creeps a few steps on hands and knees, stops and arches and hollows its back a couple of times in succession.

3. Next the cat bends backwards as far as it can until its bottom reaches its heels.

4. The cat breathes three times and during each exhalation it sounds its most beautiful 'miaow'.

5. Now the cat sniffs the ground for something nice to eat and hollows its back as low as possible. Both hands flat on the ground, slightly ahead of the chest, elbows crooked.

6. Slowly the cat rises slightly and elbows stretch.

7. The cat will now arch and hollow its back a couple of time, stop and raise a paw to wash its head.

8. Then suddenly it leaps high, if there is a climbing frame on the wall, it climbs up quickly and miaows again right at the top.

❀ **Guinea-pig maze**

The variation theme belonging to cats is Cats, Guinea-pigs and Fish. Look at the silly guinea-pigs running around until they collapse...

This is a kind of game you can play in many different ways and you can invent all kinds of rules yourself. We use coloured pencils.

In turns child A and child B place a couple of squares or oblongs which are open on one side. They can be placed at random but they should not touch each other. A few more open squares are added in another colour and this we repeat another couple of times. Finally child A and B draw joined-up lines in turn, thus creating a maze. Some random numbers of one or two digits are placed in the Maze. They could be big, small, wide and narrow numbers, on a little road or beside a little road. Discuss together how you would like to do this. You could also add several figures or objects in the Maze, for example a piece of cheese, a bowl of water, a cream cake... with a number.

Red numbers will become penalty points later on.

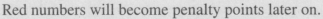

Child A is the cat and wears the eye mask or blindfold. Child B is the guinea-pig. The guinea-pig runs through the Maze in very small loops on its little paws. Suddenly the cat will say 'stop'! and at that moment the guinea-pig is not allowed to run anymore. Where did it stop, at which number? Its paws in the butter, or in the cream cake?

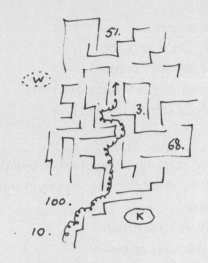

You could also use a ruler to measure the distances. You could agree for instance not to move more than half a centimetre away from the number or object.

Calculate your score. You need to deduct the red numbers! You could take turns being a guinea-pig or be one three times running. Do be fair about stopping. Have fun!

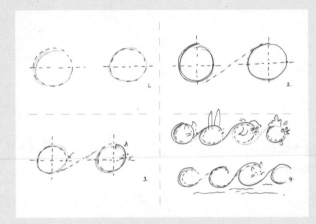

Foundation drawing

Story drawing

Text	Movements in the air
Chorus Miaow, miaow, Raw fish is my chow, but catfood even better. So juicy and so healthy and sound, my belly is now full and round.	1. Wash head and paws 2. Stroke your tummy
We're sneaking on our tiptoes tonight And we're keeping the skipper in sight (miaow) He gives us a stroke and a biscuit or two	Indicate creeping movements with your arms
We swallow it up for me and for you	Indicate with your hands that you are gulping down food
Miaow, miaow, Raw fish is my chow, but catfood even better. So juicy and so healthy and sound, my belly is now full and round.	Repeat
But the little mouse in his tiny hole Just won't come And we lose all control	Two forefingers stretched together like an extended nose
A spider we chase around up and down We are going wild... Playing the clown.	Make grabbing and skipping movements
Miaow, miaow, Raw fish is my chow, But catfood even better. So juicy and so healthy and sound, My belly is now full and round.	Repeat

Write Drawing	Illustrations
1. Draw two big circles and immediately draw three quarters circles around them If you want to, quickly add eyes, ears and whiskers 2. Stroke your tummy	
Draw krongelidong loops along the sides	
Indicate while holding the chalk in your hand that you are gulping down the food	
1. Three quarter circles 2. Take the tip of the sponge across eyes, ears and whiskers	
Trace arches on top of each other from side to side	
Draw dots everywhere	
Three quarter circles Trace the lines with your fingers	

The summer fete has arrived in the Write Dance village and everybody is busy making flower garlands. Doors and windows are repainted and decorated. In the orchard they hang up lights which glisten like little stars at night. The sundial in the centre of the Write Dance village is decorated with branches and bright ribbons too. The krongel-animals are also given flower garlands round their necks and their tails are plaited and dipped in white chalk dust. When they waft them the chalk flies around like snow which looks funny at the height of summer!

Boro loves the fete! He is designing an eight-leaf rollercoaster. Three water chutes are erected for the water cats. The children are allowed to try it out on their backs and they scream in delight. If you fall off, white water cat dives down immediately so that you can easily scramble back up on its back.

Milama and Jakiri, the greatest artists in the village, turn all kinds of objects into rings around the coloured sundial and the Write Dance people and children dance among them from sunrise to sunset.

Repeat of the eight foundation themes in rings round a central point

- Mandala is a word derived from Sanskrit, an old language from India, meaning 'circle'.

- Dancing the Mandala precedes Write drawing.

- We always start from a central point or the 'I-figure' in the centre...

- Straight and round lines with lots of variations continue to widen or enhance the flower or circle of rays.

- The Mandala rings are similar to the annual rings on a tree and indicate growth.

- By write drawing the Mandala we can see if the pupil has mastered the foundation movements.

Number 9 *Eight nines in a circle!*

Movements in the air

Repeating the eight music themes
Disperse in the classroom. Don't stand too close to each other because you need space to turn around and to create circles or rings around you.

I stand in the centre..., I am growing and the rays around me are making me warmer and stronger.

1. Volcano After rumbling, which we represent by stamping in a circle, we represent four powerful rays around us with our arms, when we hear the rolling tones, in and out, away from myself far into space. We continue rumbling and continue the rays.

0.39   **2. Walk** Slowly we turn around with our wrists, arms, shoulders and hips wriggling continuously.

1.27   **3. Circles and Eights**

Circles Slowly we turn round like a big sun with our arms stretched

1.56   *Eights* We make eights with both hands, forward away from your chest in flowing, waving movements, from side to side, in and out and out and in, time and time again...

2.25   **4. Robot dance** Let the music inspire you!

2.55   **5. Train** Turn your arms around along your body like an old fashioned locomotive, alternating with loops of smoke which we make around us with our wrists.

Modern train: two fists together, making loops, forward away from your chest. We simultaneously turn around.

3.47   **6. The Tree** The young tree grows, from your toes to far above your head. The leaves grow or flutter around us.

4.16   **7. The Sea** Bobbing 'starfish' or 'octopus' arms everywhere.

5.02   **8. Cats** Circles all around, then we wash our cat's head from the neck to the nose, 'miaow'. Next we start the arched swings and wave our arms up high from side to side.

Write Drawing

Preparation on paper or on the board
Look carefully and try to find the centre of the surface with your eyes. Place a dot there. Next you fold the paper in the shape of a cross and see how far the dot is from the centre. It will always be an exciting challenge! On the table board we measure the distance from the centre with our fingers and phalanxes.

The parts might be a little longer than you can fit on paper. It is important that you dare let go of the paper and continue the movements while doodling high up or low down, to then 'pick up the thread' again. After each ring we will change colours.
You could turn the paper round while write drawing, leave it, sit down or walk round your desk. You could also make the Mandala on a piece of paper that has been pre-cut in a circle.

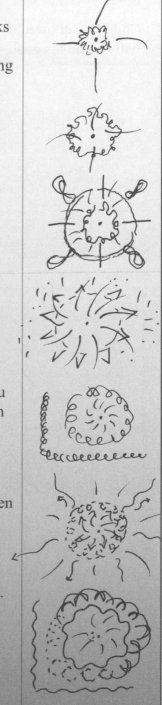

1. Volcano In the centre we first stipple or mess about with some chalks or crayons, which then change into four powerful rays in and out. Always let your piece of chalk or crayon end in the air, don't make the rays too long because there are more to follow. We will continue messing.

2. Walk We will let the chalk or crayon wriggle in all directions, on the surface but also doodling just above the surface.

3. Circles and Eights

Circles We recognise the circle music which invites us to consolidate several rings around the previous creations.

Eights We will do the same with the eights, in and out and back again. They will turn into beautiful petals or maybe the light flames of a star..

4. Robot dance Angles, dashes or dots all around.

5. Train 'Loops-around'. If you have made enough train loops, then you could also frame the board or paper with loops. Don't forget to let the train ride in the air occasionally.

6. The Tree We put the pieces of chalk or the crayons on the dot in the centre and first we let the young plant doodle upward several times and then it becomes rays using a little pressure.
The trunk and the branches become rays all around.

7. The sea Low or high waves in rays or in rings around, or as a frame.

8. Cats First draw circles round the previous creations, then swing around in 'running' arches or ocean waves. Now it is useful to rotate the paper or walk round your desk in a circle.

❀ Football game

This most exciting football game is best played on the blackboard or the tableboard.
Add a big oblong as a football field with two goals.

Child A is the goalkeeper and represents the hostile football team. Child B places its players in the field by means of dots or crosses. It is the players' job to make the ball roll in loops, from side to side in all directions, even making mock attacks.

Keeper A is not allowed to stop, and dribbles nervously to and fro in looped movements in the goal.

Watch out!... B's shot is heading for the goal in a straight line! A shoot out line. The keeper can stop the ball by bumping hands or chalk. If the line goes over the goal line, of course it is a goal!

Child B is allowed to aim at the goal five times and then the roles are reversed and child B will defend his goal.

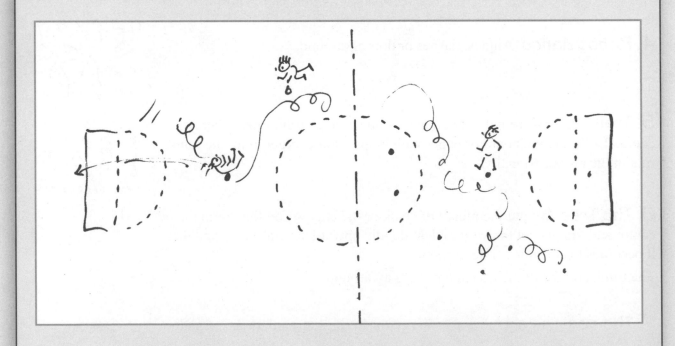

❀ **Round and straight**

Two children make a Mandala together, to the Mandala-music or by melodies, rhythms or singing words which accompany the write drawing.

Each child chooses three colours, for instance the colours of his/her clothes. Child A only draws straight lines and child B only draws round lines. Then children A and B invent many new ways to turn the variation theme into mandalas or rosettes.

Foundation drawing

Story drawing

Text	Movements in the air
I am a star, I am a sun I write a rose, that's so much fun	Dancing in circles
We dance in squares, we dance around	Dancing in circles
My head stays cool,	Hands to your head
my body sound	Arms stretched in the air or embracing yourself

Text	Movements in the air
Dancing is fine Make up a line	Dancing in circles
A krongel there and a kringelbeast A kringel, krangel, krongelbeast	Stop and wriggle your arms
We sing - loud and bold	Hold your arms to your mouth like a horn
For our story now is told!	Arms stretched up in the air

Write Drawing	Illustrations
Dance and leave the occasional krongel-squiggle on the board.	
Krongelidong around	
Hand to your head	
Arms stretched up in the air	

Write Drawing	Illustrations
Krongelidong around	
Quickly draw a krongelidong-animal	
Turn round to the audience and hold your hands to your mouth like a horn	
Arms stretched up in the air	

Variation themes

"Five, four, three, two, one, zero - go!" The enormous scaffolding which has supported the Nariana for months falls and an enormous amount of fire with lots of smoke emerges at the bottom of the rocket. It looks like a reversed volcano!

Slowly and stately rocket Nariana rises up into space. The spectators watch until it is no more than a little speck. In the space centre they watch what is happening inside the cockpit on a big screen.

"Hello Nariano, can you hear me?" a voice calls from earth. At first there is no reply but then fortunately we hear Calinco's voice, the first astronaut.

"Yes everything is fine on board - over!" The people are laughing at the floating astronauts, swimming like fish in the cockpit because when you are so far from earth, the firm ground you stand has gone. Now the hatch opens and Galinco is ready for his space walk. He is attached to a long line so that he can breathe and keep in touch with the rocket. He looks like a robot wrapped up in 20 rubber rings!

Then he suddenly sees the earth, oh how beautiful, but he has to go back in, so that the rocket can begin its return journey. What a pity, it is so beautiful in the big universe! Nariana comes down with a thud on the ice of the South Pole. To their great surprise they are met by nosy penguins.

	Movements in the air	Write Drawing
	We stand in a circle or across the hall. First try the preparatory movements without music.	*Draw two simple launchers. one upward and one downward and one round ball for the earth.*
	Motor We stamp our feet.	Quick little dashes to and fro with one or both hands at the bottom of the rocket. The feet are allowed to join in too!
0.16	**The launch** Let your arms bob from the bottom upward.	Slow bobbing waves from the bottom upward on the left and right of the launched rocket.
0.23	**Cockpit** Arms float in slow motion and twiddle knobs and dials.	Draw several instruments or slowly twisting lines to represent floating astronauts.
1.03	**Earth** With both arms we make two big circles or turn ourselves around slowly in a circle. Together: we form a big circle holding hands.	We consolidate the round ball several times or add imaginary continents.
1.45	**Return** Take a deep breath and hold it a second. Let the air escape slowly while you let your hands and your body descend slowly.	Lines bobbing slowly from the top downward past the descending rocket.
1.57	**Descent on the South Pole** Bang! Your arms should be thrown up in the air with force and making bobbing movements.	The rocket has drilled a hole in the ice. We Write Draw this hole with jagged lines.
2.06	**Penguins** Holding our hands tightly against the body we shuffle along like penguins.	Dashes approaching the 'hole'.

Rocket **CD 22** Variation theme

Write-drawing rhyme and Exercises on lines

Three, two, one, zero

Fire! ... and off we go   Draw lines, stamp and shake

High, high in the sky

We feel happy and free

Like a buzzy-li-bee
                                 Waves and hands upwards
What a beautiful sight

Is this shining and sparkling light!   Dots and dashes all around

Music drawing

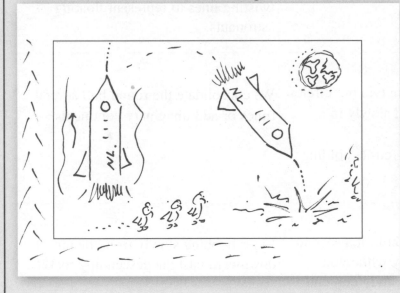

We can add our own decorative borders to the music drawing in the variation themes. The width of the decorative border is just as big as your thumb. Measure the distance along the edges several times with your thumb and place dots. You can join the dots for instance by means of a beautiful wavy line but also with a ruler. You may decorate the decorative border during the music but you could also do it afterwards, singing or humming.

Decorative border in the music drawing

Penguins To our great surprise the penguins come to meet the astronauts. The decorative border shows this in flat slanting dashes or walk across your drawing on stretched finger tips first.

Combine this theme with the Volcano. We float to the Volcano-planet in our capsule.

During the next flight the Nariana capsule floats silently through space. The astronauts enjoy the silence and the varied colours blue, orange and yellow around them. In the distance they see stars and planets and they tell the space centre on earth about everything they see.

"Didos, are you ready to open the front hatch?" the voice on earth asks them. "Yes, I am completely ready! Over," answers Didos, the second astronaut. And there he goes just like Calinco. So proud to experience this.

"Didos what can you see at this moment?" the voice from earth asks. "I see…, I see…, something that looks like our Nariana! Another rocket! It is made of shiny metal with two square flaps and it looks like gold. It is now approaching slowly. Shall I wait so that I can see everything a bit better?"

"Go straight back to the Nariana, Didos, leave navigation to us. I think we will return to earth as quickly as possible!" And Didos is very sorry.

Movements in the air	Write Drawing
Floating capsule and planets We lie on the floor very quietly and listen with our eyes closed to the music lasting three minutes which tells us what may happen in space. Keep rolling over carefully as if you are a floating capsule and tell everytingl you see in a soft voice, using your hands and fingers.	This exercise we do while sitting. Put on the eye mask or close your eyes. First let you arms float around you in the writing space and be inspired by the music into... volcano-planets, stars, satellites, solar panels, or maybe a Write Dance city...?

Music drawing

Decorative border in the music drawing
Krongel-wriggly lines with dots, dashes and stars. We will try to find some regularity in it. The teacher might draw one or two examples of this on the big board. Don't forget to hum!

Combine this theme with the foundation theme Walk; first we walk over the earth then we float in space.

Write-drawing rhyme and Exercises on lines

Flying and floating so far	Krongel-lines
I can see the volcano star	Draw quickly a volcano
Rocks and steam downward tumble	
Thunder, light and lava rumble	
She is so very very old ...	
And never feels cold!	Draw a star

Schrijfdans © 2008   Oefening op regels 2 Ruimtewandeling

I went to an island which hardly anybody had visited. It is where you can find the most improbable flowers. The most beautiful flower I saw there was a beautiful red flower and quite unique in its kind. I called her Freya, the most noble queen flower. She was as big as my hand and while I was drawing her something very special happened. She bent over as if she wanted to see my drawing and she spread a wonderful scent. Suddenly some twenty beetles in a variety of colours crept out of the queen flower, all beautifully in line. They crept over my pen and my hand and danced across my drawing. I couldn't believe my eyes. Was I dreaming or did this actually happen? When the dance had finished they all flew back together to queen Freya who immediately closed her big leaves.

When I had finished my drawing the whole scene repeated itself: the flower bent over gracefully, the beetles pattered out again, on to my drawing pad, did a dance and flew back again. I still can't believe how this was possible.

Movements in the air	Write Drawing

Flowers in the wind

The pupils disperse in the classroom and represent different flowers. They move slowly in the wind.
One or two children dance gracefully round a chosen flower. Boys, too, can learn to dance gracefully!

It would be best to do this music drawing sitting down, unless you would like to make one or two big flowers, which you make bigger and bigger by consolidating them, but of course this is also possible with smaller flowers.

0.39
0.49
0.52
0.54
0.57
1.05
1.07
1.10
1.12

Ladybirds

Very light triangle sounds represent the ladybirds...
Fingertips patter over the floor or on the table surface but also over your clothes.

We only use some light pressure to draw small circles, dashes or dots when we hear the triangle sounds. And then they have gone completely.

Music drawing

To prepare for the flowers draw a couple of big and small crosses over the surface, with or without circles. You could also make them into double crosses with lines in various lengths. We sketch a couple of small circles in another colour to represent the ladybirds.

We make flowers in all kinds of shapes and sizes. Some petals fly up doodling high in the air!

Decorative border in the music drawing

While humming, draw circles in pairs with a little distance between them to make groups of horizontal or vertical eights. First we connect them in one colour, then in another colour in a long chain. Only in the corners do you lift up your finger or writing tool.

Combine this theme with the foundation theme Circles and Eights and turn it into a wonderful expression of dancing and drawing.

Write-drawing rhyme and Exercises on lines

Have you ever seen	Draw an eight-leaf clover
Freya the Flower Queen?	
She is as big as your hand	
The noblest of this land	Draw rays all around
Beetles flying out and in	
Their wings, so light and thin	Dots in lines, in and out!

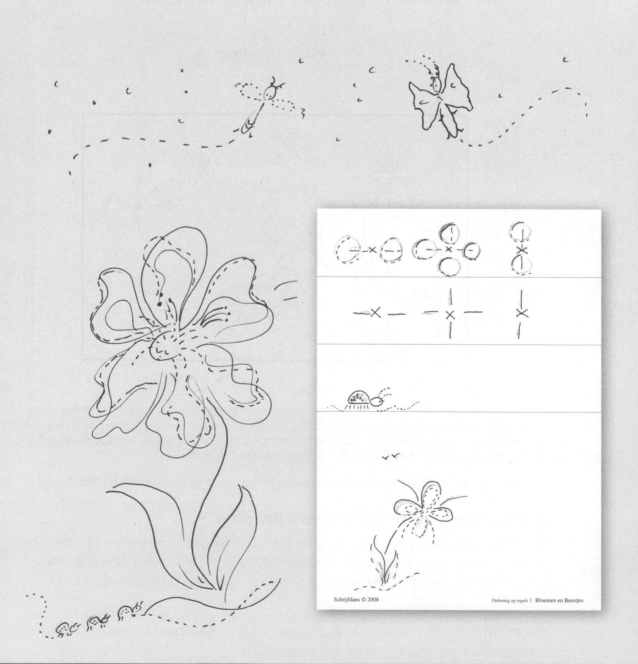

Schrijfdans © 2008   Oefening op regels 3 Bloemen en Beestjes

Boro is back in Robot land. His family is so pleased to see him back that they have organised a party for him. The best kinds of oils are taken from the cupboard: lubricating oil, diesel oil, olive oil, palm tree oil, sunflower oil... It makes the robots feel like moving, squeaking, flashing all their cogs, hinges and lids. They dance until deep in the night!

 "Where have you been my son?" asked his father between the robot dances, "We sent so many signals to you but you didn't signal back!"

"Dear father, the doors of the houses in the Write Dance village are so low that I often bumped my head which repeatedly caused a short circuit in my steel body. It would take days before I had repaired myself and got everything going again. But you know, father, the Write Dance people need us. Their village has grown into a small city and there is a lot of technical work that needs doing. Are you coming back with me?"

"Yes, but how far do we have to walk, Boro, are there enough robot oil trees on the way to fill up?" "Plenty father, trust me!" And thus they all went on their way. Far in the distance you could hear their heavy footsteps, squeaks and sounds.

Movements in the air	Write Drawing
Big and little robots, squeaks and crackles... We follow each other leaving some space between each other, all expressing what they hear and feel.	Draw freely or design figures, everything is possible: straight and slanting lines, squares and triangles, flowers and wheels, big and small...
Robots and flowers Switch on the flower music (CD 6 or 24) at a suitable moment. The robots sniff the beautiful flowers They open and close and after a couple of seconds they change back into robots and continue their journey.	Don't forget to sit down and stand... and sit and stand... to the beat of the music while you are write drawing and continue to draw lines. We draw circles and eights all around us or propellers.
Variations in the music Gentle music: we tiptoe and make very small movements. Louder music: the movements increase.	Small and big dashes, dots and quick circles or big long dashes over each other.

Music drawing

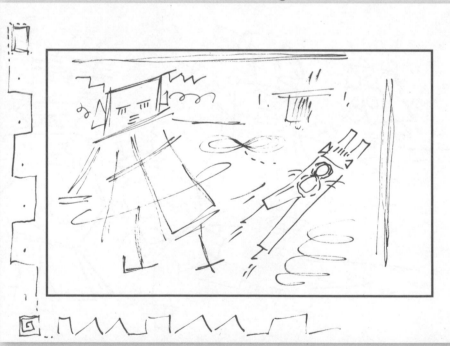

Decorative border in the music drawing
Dashes, squares, triangles. Detach the paper and rotate it or walk round your desk.

Combine this theme with the foundation theme Circles and Eights and turn it into a beautiful expression of dance!

Write drawing-rhyme and Exercises on lines

Teeny, weeny, tiny tot

Could you be a robot   Draw two squares

Now, let us march in pairs   Two more squares, angles linking

Up and down the stairs   Draw the stairs over the angles

Look how smashing

Our lids are flashing!   Circles and dashes all around

Schrijfdans © 2008   Oefening op regels 4 Robotoptocht

Choo, choo, choo, puff, puff, puff, the locomotive with five wagons is working hard. Very slowly he crawls up the mountain and then races across the plain. The people enjoy the beautiful views, snow-capped mountain peaks, woods and lakes, but then the train suddenly slows down and comes to a halt. Two brown cows with curly horns are lying across the track and they are determined not to get up. Then two cowboys arrive galloping with cracking whips. They laugh in response to the train driver who is waving. Maybe it is the first time for this to happen. The cowboys fling their lassoes round the cows' horns and carefully pull the animals off the track.

The train driver boards his train to continue. This time it is three Indians racing towards them on white-brown flecked horses, stopping at the train. They indicate that they are their cows. But the cowboys do not look convinced. There is a long discussion with many gestures. It goes on for ever and the passengers are impatient.

Finally the cows are returned to the Indians ceremoniously and they smoke the peace pipe. The passengers were very excited but also relieved that it all ended well. "Right folks, all on board, this delay has taken long enough," says the conductor and throws a big shovel of coal on the fire.

Cowboys and Indians	CD 26, 27	Variation theme

	Movements in the air	Write Drawing
CD 26	**Trudging horse** We are cowboys and are relaxed in how we sit in the saddle: on your chair or behind each other on the PE bench. The landscape is a wide expanse with numerous cactuses, the sun is warm and the horse trudges along. Feet on the ground and only heels moving up and down to the slow tempo of the music. Don't forget to keep shoulders and necks relaxed and to move them along. Sing or whistle the melody or clack your tongue.	This is suitable music for arcades and arches. First we trace the walking arches over each other to express the trudge. If we draw the arches in a long row, in similar or different sizes, together they will create the fence of a ranch. As separate loose arches they will be horseshoes. Next we also make garlands: The cowboy shuffles to and fro in his saddle.
1.08	**Gallop and lassoes** Yo-ho! Now the pace increases, let the lassoes crack and spin and swing them over the buffaloes' horns, grazing somewhere in the classroom. Alternate this with a gallop. You move your bottom up and down and hold the reins tightly.	Draw circles with two dashes for horns everywhere and add a few numbers. Close your eyes and let your lasso doodle high up in the air to 'catch' a buffalo.

Music drawing

CD 27	**Indians** Turn it into a real Indian dance!
	Decorative border in the music drawing Trudging, lassoes or Indian dashes, or a combination of all three. Singing, humming and stamping! **Combine** this Wild-West theme with the Train, the Rain Forest or the Guinea-Pigs: some small foals are joining in!

Write drawing rhyme and Exercises on lines

Cool cowboys cantering from afar	Garlands or arcades shuffle and sway forward
Coming from the dessert, here we are	
We make our lassoes spin and swing	
'Cause we are not afraid of anything!	Circling and doodling high

Schrijfdans © 2008　　　　Oefening op regels 5　Cowboys en Indianen

I have already told you about the beautiful island where I met the queen flower. I just couldn't forget about her and I returned to the island. I searched for hours in the deep rain forest and finally could not find the way back along the meandering paths. "Cahcah... cahcah," said a cockatoo as if she were laughing at me. Desperate and exhausted I sat on the ground and ate my cheese and lettuce sandwich.

Suddenly there was this big gorilla standing next to me, powerfully beating its chest. I froze with fear and without thinking I lay my sandwich at its feet. He picked it up immediately, smelled it and devoured it in one gulp. Then a wonderful thing happened. The gorilla stretched its long arms towards me and without thinking I placed my hand in his giant hand. Interestingly I no longer felt afraid. At that point he became my friend and he carefully led me through the dense forest. After a while I saw the white sands in the distance. Wasn't I happy to see my little boat! My friend the gorilla turned back and disappeared into the jungle as quickly as he had appeared.

I am sure you understand that I have begun to love this fairytale island and that I have returned many times.

Movements in the air	Write Drawing

Trees and leaves

Similar to the space walk we now lie quietly on the floor with our eyes closed, listening to the music and the sounds, accompanying them with our voices, hands and fingers.

At a suitable moment we walk through the classroom and feel surrounded by the rain forest. Push back branches, cut lianas, be frightened by a tiger which suddenly pops up in front of you... very exciting!

We put on the eye mask and sketch the Rain forest in a couple of quick lines with little pressure and in plain grey. We use the helping hand because it can't press too hard.

Slide the eye mask over your head and choose two colours for the trees and the thick foliage. Make another quick sketch. Select one or two additional colours and pull the eye mask back over your eyes. Now draw the leaves and trees with your helping or writing hand but only apply light pressure.

Music drawing

Decorative border in the music drawing

First circles, then leaves in bobbing lines. Join them together in another colour. Colour them in different colours and draw the leaf nerves.

Combine this theme with the foundation theme The Tree, Circles and Eights, the Sea or the Pleasure Boat for streams, rivers and lakes or combine with the Cats for the tigers, pumas and leopards.

Write drawing rhyme and Exercises on lines

I am at my best

In an Indian rain forest

I sit on an elephant

Swaying and swinging, it's elegant

Greeting Eeny-Meeny-Miny-Mo

Can she too have a little go?

Draw at first an elephant with you on top

Swaying and swinging garlands

Put her in your elephant basket!

Schrijfdans © 2008   Oefening op regels 6 Regenwoud

135

The long boat lay waiting by the quay until everybody had boarded. They were elderly people in a wheelchair or holding onto a walking frame. It was their day's outing in the river boat on the big river, which meanders through the hills with lots to see. After three long hoots the ship left the quayside slowly and travelled up the river. It was a wonderful sunny day and the long narrow boat with at least a hundred windows slid majestically and almost noiselessly down the wide river. There was a little orchestra on board and some carers did a little dance. Other carers had brought big sheets of paper, crayons and sticky tape because they were going to write dance with the elderly people.

"Play a march for us, then we can play robots!" the head carer said cheerfully. The grandpas and grandmas were having fun! Some of them were stamping their feet behind their walking frames but others picked up the pieces of crayon immediately. They drew lines, angular shapes, diamonds and mountain tops and forgot their ages.

Mr Hammer drew a robot and occasionally danced with his pieces of crayon in the air. "This write dance drawing is for my grandson who will be six tomorrow!" he said proudly and then everybody was given coffee and hot cocoa with cake, but Mr Hammer asked for a big sheet of drawing paper because he couldn't give up write dancing.

Movements in the air	Write Drawing
The river Music by B. Smetana, 'The Moldau' The pleasure boat is ready to leave. The last few boxes are being loaded and the ropes are released. We act it out. There it goes... the journey is ready to take off. We follow each other in a bobbing line or invent variations.	Draw a quick sketch of hills, trees and villages with your helping or writing hand, using light pressure. Now we switch on the music and the river meanders through the light sketches.
Reed and dancing We squat and first we bounce up and down a couple of times, then we stand up and bend our wrists in turn to the beat of the music.	We alternate drawing two dashes on the surface and two in the air. Carefully alternate left and right. Write draw and dance simultaneously.
Rapid Oh dear, the river suddenly changes into a very fast stream, we pass a waterfall and ...	High waves in the air and on the surface: with some light pressure on your entire write drawing or somewhere on a suitable spot.
The lake / the quay ... fortunately it ends well and we glide safely towards a big lake or the quay where we disembark.	Calm waves and ripples everywhere or somewhere on the surface.

Time markers (left column): 0.43, 1.42, 2.24, 2.59

Music drawing

Decorative border in the music drawing
Waves and waves, big ones and small ones...

Combine this theme with the Sea / Silver Wings or the Rain Forest.

Write drawing rhyme and Exercises on lines

Hobbeli bobbeli, kabbeli kah   Draw at first a boat

The name of my boat is Hurrah

Kabbeli babbeli, bobbeli beam

She travels down the stream   Waves

Wind and waves here and there   High waves

My boat tumbles everywhere

Schrijfdans © 2008   Oefening op regels 7   De Rivierboot / Plezierboot

This year the Olympic Games for pets were organised for pets in the city of Lumbushabah somewhere in the centre of Africa. The stadium is a very special building. The outer ring is an aquarium, in which the fish swim in circles as fast as they can.

All kinds of races are held on the lawn in the centre. The guinea pigs run around in their maze and need to stop quite often when they are exhausted. There are high jumps and long jumps for the cats. The sleek Morima from South America jumped as far as 3 meter 10 and broke her own world record! Other animals were represented as well. The dogs played a football tournament. The finale was between the boxers and the Dalmatians. It was an exciting match which was decided in the final minute by an excellent header by the Dalmatian County. I could tell you so much more about all that happened but I guess you will have read it in the newspaper.

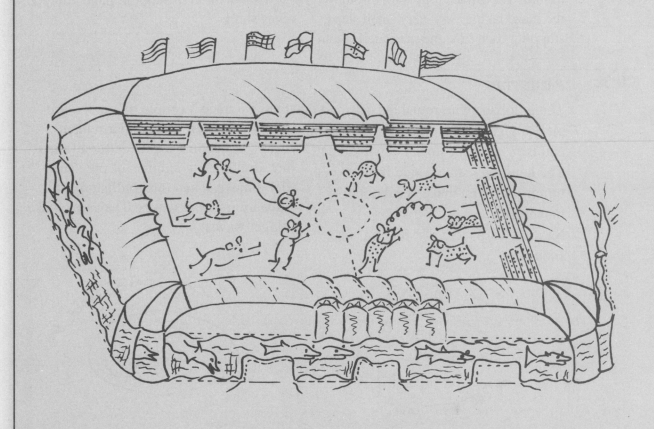

	Movements in the air	Write drawing
	We form three groups: Cats, Guinea Pigs and Fish.	
CD 30 0.23 0.37 ± 1.06	### Cat jumps high and far The cats' terrain is in the centre of the hall. They jump as high as possible and try to catch a fly. Then they continue stalking. They jump as far as they can to catch a mouse. Eventually they stop to wash themselves.	Arches from side to side, over and across each other. High jumps mean that your hand flies straight up in the air. Close your eyes quickly and let your hand descend. Long jumps mean that your arm shoots forward in a curve. Again close your eyes quickly and your arm falls on the paper. Where have you landed? On top of the guinea pigs, in the mud or maybe in the aquarium?
CD 31	### Guinea-pig maze We make a maze with boxes and little boxes, counter-pieces and objects, shawls and skipping ropes around the cats' terrain. The guinea pigs walk through the maze taking very, very small steps, stopping each time the music tells them to.	The guinea pigs run round in tiny little loops and stop dead when the music tells them to. Try this with your helping hand and your eyes shut!
CD 32	### Aquarium The goldfish swim round the cats and the guinea pigs. First we move by swimming and then we walk slowly down the hall. The hands are stretched in front of your tummy and first make small bobbing movements. Next the carps join in with arms and shoulders.	First we trace a couple of small waves over each other. They either remain waves or become eights. After all, fish are afraid of big animals of prey and don't move. Then the goldfish move forward in small waves. The carps make bigger waves.
	### Decorative border in the music drawing The guinea pigs might be given huts and the fish feel safe with the sharks.	
	Combine this theme with the foundation theme Cats, Rain Forest, Walk, Space walk, the Sea and the Pleasure Boat, each theme independently or all in succession. It has become quite a performance!	

Write drawing rhyme and Exercises on lines

Just like an Olympic stadium we draw a big oval on our paper.
In order to do so we first fold the paper in the shape of a cross. Next we fold the
two corners towards the centre. We draw an arch round each diagonal folding line.
Consolidate it a couple of times, to and fro, again and again. Then draw one oval for
the fish and one for the guinea pigs.

Music drawing

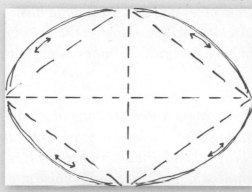 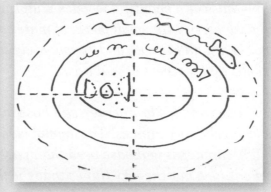

My cat can jump as high as Big Ben	Draw at first your cat, Big Ben and the Thames
but then...	
He doesn't want to come down again	
said my uncle Brown	
But finally he jumped in the Thames	
said my nephew Benz	Eyes closed while jumping!

Schrijfdans © 2008   Oefening op regels 8 Katten, Cavia's en Vissen

141

The Mandala party was such a great success that the mayor of the Write Dance city decided to repeat the party in spring. Anyone can submit their ideas and designs to the civic centre and a jury will determine the winner.

Bo Balimo has cut a beautiful wooden sculpture from pinewood and Ka Kalima has created a tapestry with small pieces of material. Aroldo is still working on the drawing of a mother bear and her cub, and Takoro and Salina have designed costumes incorporating small shells and feathers of seabirds.

Boro the robot and his brother are still busy building a complicated washing machine for the krongelidong-animals. The animal is meant to stand in a kind of washhouse and within ten minutes it will have been shampooed, brushed and dried with hot air. It is an excellent idea but the jury thinks that the machine still makes too much noise and therefore the robot brothers are looking for a better solution.

Stein the blacksmith has made something very special and won the first prize. He is allowed to produce a large copy of his design for the spring party. He will place a roof on top of the sun post in stained glass in a variety of different colours. The roof can turn slowly and when the sun shines you see the most beautiful colours around the post. The jury named it the Write Dance Rosette.

	Movements in the air	Write drawing
	As in the foundation theme Mandala all eight themes return briefly. 'I am a rose and I continue opening my petals. I am growing and my colour is becoming stronger, spreading a wonderful scent... *First fold or divide the paper into a vertical and a diagonal cross. Then draw a circle. Do let go, otherwise the rosette will be too full. So don't forget to doodle at high and low level while write drawing.*	
	1. Rocket Stamping in a circle	1. Squiggling to and fro
0.17	**2. Space walk** Letting your arms float while rotating slowly	2. Krongelidong-lines
0.51 1.26	**3. Flowers and Ladybirds** Arms form horizontal eights, from your chest outward and back in again	3. Lying and standing eights
1.42	**4. Robot procession** Big steps around and wrists up and down	4. Lines, dashes, angles and squares
2.27 2.53 3.25	**5. Trudging, lassoes and Indians** We trudge along on our horses Indian dance	5. 'Swaying saddles'
3.59	**6. Rain Forest** Snakes crawl, monkeys jumps	6. Waves and little jumps
4.45	**7. The River / Pleasure boat** Hands and wrists make waves and ripples	7. Big and small waves
5.22 5.51 6.05	**8. Cats, guinea pigs and fish** Cat-swings and cat jumps Guinea pig patters Goldfish waves	8. 'Running' arches from side to side
	Decorative border in the music drawing Everything is possible!	

Write drawing rhyme and Exercises on lines

My rosette is the prettiest rose

She is the flower I chose

For my Write Dance drawing

Ring-a-ling-ding-ding-ding

My head stays cool

My body sound

Will you dance this little round?

Draw at first a rosette flower...

Circling around

... and around

Hands on your head

Arms crossing over your breast

Music drawing

NOTES

Write Dance Training

'In Write Dance music is the power and the motor which makes all written expressions move!'

To find out about dates and availability, contact **Ragnhild Oussoren** or **Diana Strauss** on the e-mails listed below.

Day one: Write Dance in the Early Years and Write Dance
10.00–15.00 or 9.00–14.00 coffee break and lunch included.

We start with movements 'in the air', on the table with senso-motorical materials, on the tableboard with chalks and on large sheets of paper with crayons. By so called 'scrimbling' we will make drawings of nursery songs especially composed for children 3–5. Supporting child-initiated play within the foundation curriculum and the 'Birth to Three Matters' framework, these provide an introduction to the nine themes in Write Dance approach at an appropriate developmental level.

After the coffee break we continue with Write Dance for ages 4–8. From scrimbling we progress into writemoving which results in musicdrawings accompanied by classical and popular music. The Write Dance movements provide the children with a strong foundation for writing, and help them to feel happy and comfortable with their bodies. The book and CD resource provides everything the early years practitioner needs to implement this exciting approach.

Day two: More Write Dance

Extending the development of Write Dance for children aged 4–8.
The theory and the philosophy are explained in much greater depth, and more music, instructions and illustrations are provided to guide and inform teachers and children on how to move and 'move-draw' to refine and to develop their movements and their drawings to achieve fluent letter strings, with ease and speed.

Ragnhild Oussoren worked for many years as a consultant graphologist in the Netherlands and in Sweden. Mixing her graphology skills with art and music, in the 1990s she developed a completely new writing and movement method for all children aged 3–12 years irrespective of their movement skills. The Write Dance method has been so successful that it is practised in seven languages and in many countries.

Write Dance Workshops are available from the author, Ragnhild Oussoren. Contact Ragnhild at info@schrijfdans.nl

Also available in the UK are Write Dance Workshops with Diana Strauss.

Diana Strauss can provide practical Write Dance workshops from 'Write Dance in the Early Years' to 'Write Dance and 'More Write Dance'. Whole day, half-day and twilight workshops are available. Sessions can include children and their parent/carers. Please wear sensible footwear and comfortable clothes.

Contact Diana Strauss at dswritedance@aol.co.uk to book a session!